HISTORY DETECTIVES

Prehistoric Peoples

Prehistoric Peoples

Discover the ancient world of the first human beings

Philip Brooks

southwater

This edition is published by Southwater

Distributed in the UK by
The Manning Partnership
251–253 London Road East
Batheaston
Bath BA1 7RL
tel. 01225 852 727
fax 01225 852 852

Published in the USA by
Anness Publishing Inc.
27 West 20th Street
Suite 504
New York
NY 10011
fax 212 807 6813

Distributed in Canada by
General Publishing
895 Don Mills Road
400–402 Park Centre
Toronto, Ontario M3C 1W3
tel. 416 445 3333
fax 416 445 5991

Distributed in Australia by
Sandstone Publishing
Unit 1, 360 Norton Street
Leichhardt
New South Wales 2040
tel. 02 9560 7888
fax 02 9560 7488

Southwater is an imprint of Anness Publishing Limited
Hermes House, 88–89 Blackfriars Road, London SE1 8HA
tel. 020 7401 2077; fax 020 7633 9499

© Anness Publishing Limited 2000, 2002

Publisher: Joanna Lorenz
Managing Editor: Gilly Cameron Cooper
Senior Editor: Lisa Miles
Editorial Reader: Joy Wotton

Produced by Miles Kelly Publishing Limited

Art Director: Clare Sleven
Project Editor: Raje Airey
Assistant Editors: Helen Parker
Design: Angela Ashton
Art Commissioning: Susanne Grant; Lynne French
Picture Research: Kate Miles; Lesley Cartlidge;
Liberty Mella; Janice Bracken

Picture Credits
The publishers would like to thank the following
artists who have contributed to this book:

James Field (SGA); Richard Hook (Linden Artists); John James
(Temple Rogers); Stuart Lafford (Linden Artists); Shane Marsh
(Linden Artists); Terry Riley; Martin Sanders; Peter Sarson;
Rob Sheffield; Sue Stitt; Mike White (Temple Rogers); John Woodcock.

All maps are by Steve Sweet (SGA)

The publishers wish to thank the following
for supplying photographs for this book:

Page 8 (B/L) AKG Photo; 9 (B) Erich Lessing/AKG London; 11 (B)
Mary Jelliffe/Hutchison Library; 16 (B/R) E.T. Archive; 18 (B/R) E.T.
Archive; 26 (B/L) The Stock Market; 28 (B/R) The Stock Market;
35 (B) Mary Jelliffe/Hutchison Library; 38 (T/R) Erich Lessing/AKG
London; 41 (B) Ancient Art & Architecture Collection; 44 (T/R)
English Heritage Photo Library; 52 (M) English Heritage Photo
Library; 55 (T) English Heritage Photo Library; 58 (T/R) English
Heritage Photo Library; 61 (B/L) Southwell/Hutchison Library.

All other photographs from Miles Kelly archives.

1 3 5 7 9 10 8 6 4 2

Previously published as *Exploring History: Prehistoric Peoples*

CONTENTS

Introduction
6

Finding the
Evidence
8

The Toolmakers
10

The Coming
of Fire
12

The Spread of
the Hominids
14

Neanderthals
16

Wise Man
18

The First
Europeans
20

The Ice Age
22

Images of
the Ice Age
24

The First
Australians
26

Early Americans
28

The Thaw Begins
30

A Better Food
Supply
32

Rock Paintings
34

The First Farmers
36

Plants and
Animals
38

The Coming
of Trade
40

Pots and
Potters
42

European
Settlements
44

Asian Communities
46

The Americas
48

Hunting and Gathering
50

The First
Metalworkers
52

Megaliths
54

Lake Villages
56

The Iron Age
58

Birth of Civilization
60

Glossary
62

Index
64

Introduction

THIS BOOK LOOKS BACK to the very beginnings of the human story. It starts at a time when people lived in caves and sheltered under cliffs, when the only tools were made of stone, when everyone had to hunt or forage for their own food, when clothes had to be made from animal skins. There were no cities, no large buildings, none of the comforts of modern life, and no one had worked out how to write. The term "prehistory" means the time before people were able to write their history down. Writing developed at different times in different parts of the world, so the date when the prehistoric period ended varies from one place to another. In Mesopotamia in Southwest Asia, for example, writing came around 3000B.C. In western Europe, by contrast, widespread use of written scripts coincided with the Roman conquerors around 3,000 years later.

Prehistoric life can sound grim. Life was hard, travel must have been difficult, and many people died young without the benefits of effective medicine. Yet the period sees the beginnings of the very things that make humanity what it is today. Technology was simple, but it made possible amazing monuments such as Stonehenge. Artists had only basic materials, yet they produced masterpieces on cave walls. People cared for

▲ HOMINIDS
The first human-apes appeared about four million years ago in Africa. They came down from the trees where they lived and began to walk on the ground on two legs. Scientists call them australopithecines.

▼ KEY DATES
How humans and human society developed in different parts of the world.

▼ CAVE ART
It seems that humans have always felt the urge for artistic self-expression. During the Ice Age, people lived in caves. Wall paintings from that time show people's skill in making their homes colorful and attractive.

	2–1MILLION YEARS AGO	1M.Y.A.–400,000B.C.	400,000–30,000B.C.	30,000–12,000B.C.
AFRICA	Early hominids, the first human-apes, are alive in eastern Africa.	*Homo erectus*, a type of early human, use stone hand axes as a multi-purpose tool.	*Homo sapiens*, humans, appear in various places south of the Sahara.	
MIDDLE EAST & ASIA	*Homo erectus* is established in both Java and China, and has probably mastered the use of fire.		Neanderthals and "modern" humans are living side by side in Mesopotamia.	Rock painting
EUROPE		First known settlement of *Homo erectus* in Europe.	Neanderthals and "modern" humans are present, and may breed, but Neanderthals die out.	Europe freezes in the Ice Age. Artists make great cave paintings in France and Spain.
AMERICAS				The first settlement of North America begins as men and women cross the Bering land bridge from Siberia.

Skull of *Homo habilis*

Saber-toothed cat

M.Y.A.: Million years ago

their sick, using medicines made from plants, and some illnesses were cured this way.

This book looks at prehistoric life all over the world. It begins with the origins of the human race in Africa and how people spread out around the world. It tells how people developed simple tools, survival skills such as hunting and food gathering, and the ability to make clothes and simple shelters. Gradually, human activities such as art, religion, and ceremonies developed, signs that social groups were becoming more complex.

Next, the book shows the enormous progress made by early peoples, starting with the invention of pottery and the beginnings of farming, which helped men and women control their food supply. Trade then enabled more people to travel and new ideas to spread around the world. The next "revolution" was when people learned how to use metals, by working copper, making bronze, and smelting iron. Finally came the invention of writing, the development of large cities and societies, and the end of the prehistoric period. Throughout this period, people overcame tremendous obstacles, such as the huge climate changes of an Ice Age.

▲ MAMMOTH SHELTER
Homes were built from whatever materials were available. Remains of mammoth bones suggest they were used to build massive shelters almost 10 feet high.

▶ FISH CARVING
After the Ice Age, food supplies were much better. Fish carvings found in Europe suggest that fish had become part of the staple diet.

▼ WATCHTOWER
Eventually people began building permanent settlements. The walled city of Jericho dates from about 7000 B.C. and is one of the earliest cities discovered so far. It had watchtowers like this one, which were more than 30 feet high.

12,000–9000 B.C.	9000–6000 B.C.	6000–4000 B.C.	4000–2000 B.C.	2000 B.C.–A.D. 1
 Japanese pot	 Auroch, an early bull	The climate of what is now the Sahara Desert is very wet. Cattle herding is common in many parts of the region.		Cuneiform writing from Mesopotamia
The dog is domesticated in the Middle East. The first pottery is produced in Japan.	Farming is established in the Fertile Crescent.	Trading towns such as Çatal Hüyük, Turkey, begin to develop.	Potter's wheel invented; bronze-working begins; writing develops. Cities built in Mesopotamia.	
The great ice sheets begin to thaw as temperatures increase. Sea levels rise.	Clovis points	Farming spreads to eastern Europe, probably from Turkey.	Stone circles and other megalithic monuments become common in western Europe.	First ironworking transforms tools and weapons.
People in Chile build houses from wood and skins—the first evidence of shelters in the Americas.	The Clovis culture: on the Great Plains people hunt using stone-pointed spears.	Cotton plant	The farmers of Mexico domesticate the maize plant. Other crops spread through North America.	The Olmec people of Mexico build the region's first large cities.

Finding the Evidence

▲ BURIAL URN
Some prehistoric peoples cremated their dead by burning the bodies on a funeral pyre. The ashes, and sometimes the bones, of the dead person might then be buried in a pottery urn like this one.

INDING EVIDENCE ABOUT prehistory is like doing a gigantic jigsaw puzzle with most of the pieces missing. Often very little is now left of the prehistoric peoples who lived thousands of years ago. Archaeologists study every scrap of evidence they can find for clues as to how ancient peoples lived. Sometimes all that remain are a few bits of broken pottery, the foundations of some houses, or the occasional tool or weapon. Archaeologists have to learn what they can from fragments such as these.

Even when there is a big site—a stone circle, for example, or the remains of an ancient town—there are often more questions than answers. What were stone circles used for? Who ruled the first towns? How did people find out how to make bronze? Why did the cave artists paint their pictures? Questions like these still baffle archaeologists. The experts can suggest answers, but there are no certainties.

Graves can often give archaeologists some of the most fascinating clues about prehistory. They can be almost like time capsules. In many periods, it was the custom to bury a person with some of their possessions. Archaeologists call these items grave goods. These objects can tell us a great deal about the dead person's lifestyle, job, and wealth. They can also reveal something about the beliefs of the time. This is because grave goods were usually intended for use in the next world. Such finds suggest that people in prehistoric times believed in life after death. Some of the best evidence, though, comes from the bodies

◀CHAMBERED TOMB
This type of tomb, common in prehistoric Europe, often contains several burials. These reveal a lot about ancient society. For example, the grave of a ruler or chief was usually treated differently than the others. It might be more carefully constructed or contain richer goods.

DEATH AND BURIAL
Archaeologists rarely know what they will find when they excavate a grave. There may be only a skeleton, or there may be lavish grave goods also. Whatever they find, it will probably be very fragile if it has been in the ground for thousands of years.

◀ TOLLUND MAN
Bodies buried in swamps and bogs are protected from the air. Skin, hair, and even clothing can be preserved for hundreds of years. Tollund Man was found buried in a bog in Denmark, and dates from about 251 B.C.

▶ GRAVE GOODS
Items in graves often reveal evidence about the spread of technology. For example, these grave goods from a cemetery at Varna in Bulgaria show that their owners had discovered how to work metal.

▲ PASSAGE-GRAVE BURIAL MOUND
Many passage graves, from around 3,000 B.C., have been found in northern Europe. A passage leads to the tomb at the mound's center.

themselves. By looking at a skeleton, for example, a trained observer can tell roughly how old the person was at their time of death and whether that person was male or female. It is also possible to measure how tall the dead person was and to determine quite a lot about build, physical development and strength. Often, archaeologists can find out about a person's diet by studying the teeth and doing chemical analyses of the bones. Sometimes they can even say why a person died, as some illnesses, such as arthritis, can be detected from the bones.

Studying the features and contents of an ancient grave can provide enough evidence to work out the approximate date when the person was buried. Factors such as the condition of the bones, the way the person was buried, and the type of grave goods that are found with the skeleton, can help to date the burial. How deep the body lies in the ground is also a clue. The deeper it is buried, the older it is likely to be. Archaeologists working in a vertical trench, for example, can often see layers of objects in historical order, from the oldest to the most recent, almost like a timeline.

trowel

measuring pole

archaeologist drawing remains

ancient skeleton

foundations of settlement

grave goods

▶ ARCHAEOLOGICAL DIG
Archaeologists excavate an ancient site. They are working at several different levels. The skeleton is on an earlier level than the settlement above it. The archaeologists dig with care, using light tools, such as trowels and brushes, to avoid causing damage. Most importantly of all, they record in detail everything that they find.

▼ EXCAVATING GRAVES
Archaeologists have to be very careful when excavating dead bodies. This is not just because they are delicate. These are remains of real people, and they should be treated with respect. At this grave at Les Eyzies in France, archaeologists have worked slowly to remove the bones, which are at least 10,000 years old.

Dates and Dating

Prehistoric people lived thousands or even millions of years ago. However, because these people left no written records, archaeologists have to rely on other evidence to work out the dates of the remains they find. They have many ways of doing this, from studying the site of the find to using chemical analysis. Even so, nearly all the dates can only be approximate. The older the remains are, the less precise the dates are likely to be.

The abbreviations used with dates in this book are:

- M.Y.A. indicates "Million Years Ago." It is used for very ancient dates, a million or more years ago.

- B.C. indicates the number of years "Before Christ." Jesus lived 2,000 years ago, so you can work out a "number of years old" by adding 2,000 to a B.C. date.

The Toolmakers

▲ PEBBLE TOOL
Early hominids chipped away the sides of pebbles to make simple, sharp-edged tools.

Probably the biggest prehistoric mystery of all is how the human race began. Many scientists think that modern humans evolved, millions of years ago, from creatures that looked somewhat like apes. They hoped to find a missing link, part-ape and part-human, between modern humans and our animal ancestors. No one has found this missing link. But paleontologists (people who study fossils, the preserved remains of animals and plants) have discovered the remains of a group of creatures called early hominids. These are animals that share many features with humans. Hominids looked somewhat ape-like and had smaller brains than modern humans, but they walked on two legs and could make simple stone tools. Our ancestors were probably like ancient hominids.

No one has ever found a complete skeleton of an early hominid. Often all that remains is a fragment of bone or a single tooth. Scientists have tried to find out all about the hominids from such meager evidence. However, they often disagree about which species of hominid a particular find belongs to, and how the various species relate to each other.

The earliest hominids, who lived in Africa between four million and 800,000 years ago, are called the australopithecines (southern apes). They stood and walked upright, but were shorter than modern humans, standing between 3 and 5 feet tall. Their bodies had a similar shape to humans', but their flat-nosed faces looked ape-like. Their brains were much smaller than human brains, but larger than those of today's chimpanzees and gorillas.

Australopithecines probably spent most of their time on the ground. Like modern gorillas

◀ AUSTRALOPITHECUS ROBUSTUS
Stocky and ape-like, this hominid probably spent much of its time living in trees, but it came down to the ground from time to time to search for food. Like the modern chimpanzee, it probably ate plants most of the time.

HOMO HABILIS

Since Louis Leakey discovered the first specimen of *Homo habilis* in 1964, many similar remains have been found in Africa—especially in the fossil-rich beds of Kenya and Tanzania. Although it is not certain whether these creatures are direct human ancestors, they are definitely our close relatives.

▼ PREDATOR
Early hominids had to guard against fearsome meat-eaters like this saber-toothed cat. Sometimes the best escape from dangerous animals such as this was to take to the trees.

▲ A LARGER SKULL—
A LARGER BRAIN
Homo habilis had a much larger brain than the australopithecines, the southern apes. This was one reason why its discoverers decided that it should be included in the genus *Homo*, just like modern humans.

▼ A FIRM GRIP
Homo habilis had a hand that could grip objects firmly. This, together with its brain size, meant that the creature could make simple stone tools and may have been able to build basic shelters from tree branches and leaves.

pebble tool

simple brushwood shelter

and chimpanzees, they climbed trees to hide from enemies or to shelter from the rain. Remains of their teeth suggest that they ate mainly plants, plus a little meat. They probably also used the first simple tools.

In 1964, paleontologist Louis Leakey announced the discovery of the fossilized remains of a previously unknown hominid. It had a larger brain than the southern apes, so Leakey decided to place it in the genus *Homo*, the same as our own species. The fossil was 1.7 million years old, which makes it our oldest close relative. Stone tools were found near the remains, so Leakey named the fossil *Homo habilis* (handy man).

Like people today, the *Homo habilis* people probably ate quite a lot of meat, but no one knows whether they hunted animals for food or ate the

remains left by other animals. Archaeologists have found remains of stone tools next to animal bones, such as simple choppers and hammers made from pebbles. They were probably semi-nomadic, staying in an area for a little while before moving on to a new area for food. When they moved, they left their tools behind.

Hominid uses its upright stance to gather berries.

▶ "LUCY"
The most complete set of bones found belonged to a hominid that lived just over three million years ago. Archaeologists nicknamed it "Lucy." The bones show that it was a slim, possibly female, creature just over 3 feet tall. It weighed about 60 pounds and could walk upright. The slim build and upright stance suggest a more human-like creature than the other australopithecines.

▲ ROBUSTUS SKULL
The robust australopithecines had heavy skulls with massive jaws and strong ridges of bone across the brows. There were also flanges (areas of bone sticking out from the cheeks) on either side.

▲ AFRICANUS SKULL
Although Australopithecus africanus *had a more lightly built skull than* Australopithecus robustus, *it still had a heavy jawbone. No one is certain exactly how these two species were related.*

▲ OLDUVAI GORGE
One of the most important hominid sites is Olduvai Gorge, on the Serengeti Plains in East Africa. Fossils of several hominids, including *Homo habilis*, have been found there, which makes this one of the great hunting grounds in the search for human origins. The gorge contains fossilized remains ranging from 100,000 to around 2 million years old, the older fossils embedded in the deepest rocks. Scatters of tools, from crude pebbles to stone axes, lie near the bones of their makers.

Key Dates

- 3.6M.Y.A. Southern apes are present in Laetoli, northern Tanzania.

- 3 to 3.75M.Y.A. Southern apes present in Hadar, northern Ethiopia. The most famous example is known to modern archaeologists as "Lucy," a member of the species *Australopithecus afarensis*.

- 1.8M.Y.A. Lake Turkana, Kenya, is home to various hominids, including australopithecines and creatures with larger skulls.

- 1.75M.Y.A. *Robustus* australopithecines live at Olduvai Gorge, northern Tanzania.

- 1.75M.Y.A. The toolmaker *Homo habilis*, the oldest known member of our genus, lives at Olduvai Gorge.

The Coming of Fire

AROUND 1.6 MILLION YEARS AGO, A GROUP OF hominids mastered a completely new skill. They learned how to use fire, which must have brought about a huge change in their lives. Suddenly, they were able to cook food instead of eating raw meat and plants. They could keep their drafty caves and rock shelters warm in winter. The heat and flames could even be used as weapons against enemies. Fire probably gave them a safer and more comfortable life than the earlier hominids had enjoyed. The hominids who mastered fire were about 5 feet tall. They had bigger brains and longer limbs than previous hominids, more like those of modern humans. Scientists called them *Homo erectus* (upright man). The *Homo*

◀ FIRE STICK
One way early people made fire was to put dry grass on a stick called a hearth. Then they rubbed another stick against the hearth to make a spark and set the grass alight.

FOOD AND RESOURCES

With their larger brains, *Homo erectus* people were probably better at hunting and finding new types of food than previous hominids. Their travels across Africa may have been to search for new sources of food. Besides hunting animals and gathering plants, they probably killed injured animals or scavenged meat left by other predators.

▲ HACKBERRIES
Gathering nuts and fruit, such as these hackberries, provided a large part of the diet of *Homo erectus*. They had to learn by trial and error which berries were good to eat and which were poisonous.

◀ WOOLLY RHINO
The *Homo erectus* people tried eating whatever meat they killed. They may have eaten large creatures like this woolly rhinoceros, hunting them in groups and sharing the meat.

▲ EAST TURKANA
Close to the mountains and lakes of Kenya, the site of East Turkana was one of the first homes of *Homo erectus* around 1.5 million years ago.

erectus people were more advanced in other ways. They made better tools than the earlier hominids and developed a hand ax, a pointed flint tool with two sharp cutting edges. Hand axes were useful for cutting meat, so the *Homo erectus* people could butcher animals more efficiently. As a result, they may have had more incentive to develop their technology—for example, creating smaller tools such as cutting blades.

    Homo erectus people probably had more advanced social skills than earlier hominids. They may even have developed a simple language, which would have enabled them to talk to and cooperate with each other. This meant that they could perform tasks as a group, such as hunting large animals. They may have used fire in their hunting. Some archaeologists think that they lit bush fires to drive large animals into an ambush, where the creatures could be killed by a hunting group.

    Fire also enabled them to survive in colder climates. This encouraged *Homo erectus* people

to travel more widely than earlier hominids. Like *Homo habilis*, they were probably always on the move, making temporary camps as bases for hunting and gathering. Some of these homes may have been seasonal, occupied during the spring or summer when fruit, nuts, and leaves were plentiful. But *Homo erectus* people also traveled beyond their native Africa, and they were probably the first hominids to settle in Asia and Europe.

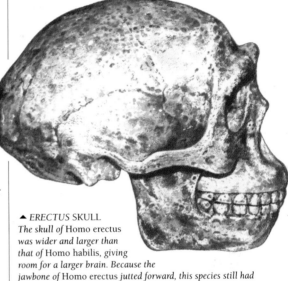

▲ *ERECTUS SKULL*
The skull of Homo erectus *was wider and larger than that of* Homo habilis, *giving room for a larger brain. Because the jawbone of* Homo erectus *jutted forward, this species still had a face that looked more like an ape's than a modern human's.*

◀ *HOMO ERECTUS*
Cave-dwelling Homo erectus people prepare to cook a meal in front of their cave. One member of the group makes stone tools, perhaps to cut up the dead animal; another tends the fire; and two children help an adult dismember the carcass before it is cooked on the hot fire.

◀ EARLY HOMINID SITES, EAST AFRICA
Most of the early remains of *Homo habilis* and *Homo erectus* have come from a cluster of sites in Kenya and Tanzania in East Africa. The structure of the rocks there has helped preserve these fossils. For example, at Olduvai Gorge, hominid bones and tools were left by the shores of a lake, later to be covered by mud and volcanic lava and preserved. Still later, geological faults caused the rocks to move, making the fossils visible.

Key Dates

- 1.6M.Y.A. The Pleistocene period begins. Animals such as horses, cattle, and elephants appear.

- 1.6M.Y.A. The earliest *Homo erectus* ever found comes from East Turkana, Kenya.

- 1.6M.Y.A. *Homo erectus* camp at Chesowanya in the Kenya Rift Valley. This shows possible evidence of the use of fire.

- 1M.Y.A. *Homo erectus* living in Olduvai Gorge.

- 500,000 years ago *Homo erectus* reaches northern Africa. Sites with evidence of *Homo erectus* have been found in Morocco and Algeria.

Map labels:
Sites of
◆ *Homo habilis*
● *Homo erectus*
N
White Nile
Omo
East Turkana ● Koobi Fora
R. Congo
L. Victoria ● Olduvai Gorge
Indian Ocean
L. Tanganyika
AFRICA
L. Nyasa
Zambezi R.
MADAGASCAR
Sterkfontein
Atlantic Ocean
0 Kilometers 1500
0 Miles 1000

The Spread of Hominids

ROUND A MILLION years ago, the world's wildlife was on the move. Many tropical animals started to travel northward and eastward. Gradually, they moved away from the sweltering jungles toward cooler parts of the globe. Food was often difficult to find for the early hominids, so the *Homo erectus* people followed the tropical animals to places with more moderate climates. In doing so, they traveled great distances, from modern Africa as far as present-day Java, China, Italy, and Greece.

In Europe and Asia, *Homo erectus* people set up camps to which they returned year after year. One of the most famous of all is a series of caves at Zhoukoudien, China. Hominids stayed here for thousands of years (from about 600,000 to about 230,000 years ago), and archaeologists have found the remains of more than 40 *Homo erectus* people at the site. In the caves the archaeologists found a variety of tools, including choppers, scrapers, awls, points, and cutters, most of which were made from quartz. The more recent

▲ A PLACE TO SHELTER
At Terra Amata, southern France, there is evidence that hominids made a camp with simple shelters. These small huts were made out of tree branches, weighted down with stones.

in date the tools, the smaller and more finely worked they are. There is also evidence of fire in the Zhoukoudien caves. Similar remains have been found in *Homo erectus* sites in Europe and Southeast Asia. They reveal a people who gathered leaves and berries but were also cunning enough to hunt large mammals. The people moved around from one season to the next. If they could not find caves, they built simple shelters from branches and stones. They probably wrapped animal skins around themselves to keep warm in the winter.

One mystery is that many surviving *Homo erectus* skulls have had their bases removed. Some scientists think that this was done so that survivors could take out the brain. Perhaps these people were the first cannibals? There may be other reasons, such as to make containers to carry water.

Another puzzle is how *Homo erectus* died out. There are no *erectus* remains later than about 200,000 years ago. It is not known whether they perished because other hominids killed them, because their food supplies ran out, or because of ill health.

ANCIENT CULTURE

The *Homo erectus* people were able to produce a wider variety of tools, weapons, and other items than the earlier hominids, although the only objects to survive in large numbers are their stone tools. They were skilled flintworkers, creating implements with razor-sharp edges for butchering meat, cutting plant food, and scraping hides. They were probably also woodworkers, using wood to build simple shelters and make weapons such as spears and clubs.

▶ PAINT
Stones marked with red ocher, a natural earth pigment, have been found at Becov in Bohemia, Europe. These finds date to 250,000 years ago and suggest that people may have decorated their bodies or items that they made. They may have mixed the ocher with fat to make a form of paint.

◀ HAND AX
The double-edged stone tool was *Homo erectus'* most common and useful implement. It fitted comfortably into the hand and was easy to carry around. The two sharp edges could be used for cutting or chopping.

◀ UPRIGHT MAN
Homo erectus people looked much like modern humans, except for their ape-like faces. But they were not as tall as most people today.

▼ ON THE HUNT
A group of Homo erectus *people have worked together to trap three elephants in a swamp. They are now about to move in on one of the animals, to attack it with wooden spears and clubs.*

swampy ground

...den spear

wooden club

0 | Kilometers | 2500 ◆ Early hominid sites **N**
0 | Miles | 1500

Swanscombe
Mauer **EUROPE**
Terra Amata   Petralona
ASIA
Zhoukoudien
CHINA
ARABIA
INDIA   Yuanmou
AFRICA   Bodo
Omo
Koobi
Olduvai Gorge   **Indian Ocean**   **JAVA**

▲ HOMO ERECTUS SITES
This successful hominid spread from Africa to both Asia and Europe. In addition to sites in China, there are also many places in Europe with early hominid remains. In the case of most of the European sites, experts are uncertain whether the occupants were *Homo erectus* or an early form of our own species.

Key Dates

- 1M.Y.A. *Homo erectus* people are established in Olduvai Gorge.

- 1M.Y.A. *Homo erectus* invents the hand ax.

- 900,000B.C. *Homo erectus* is present in central Java. The hominids' long-distance movements show them adapting to different environments.

- 700,000B.C. *Homo erectus* reaches Ubeidiya, by the Jordan and Yarmuk rivers, Israel.

- 500,000B.C. *Homo erectus* settles in Europe.

- 400,000–230,000B.C. *Homo erectus* living at Zhoukoudien Cave, near Beijing, China.

Neanderthals

▲ CAVE WOMAN
Neanderthals like this female may have been the first hominids to care for the sick and disabled. This prolonged the lives of individuals who would otherwise have met painful early deaths.

A TYPICAL CAVE MAN IS usually portrayed as a stocky creature with heavy bones, a thick ridge across the brows, and a blank expression on his face. As far as we can tell, the Neanderthals, who lived in Europe and the Middle East 70,000 to 35,000 years ago, did look somewhat like this. They are our closest relatives among the hominids and were intelligent, with brains a similar size to our own. In fact, the Neanderthals were so similar to modern humans that some scientists place them in our own species, giving them a subspecies (*Homo sapiens neanderthalensis*). Others give them a species of their own (*Homo neanderthalensis*).

The Neanderthal people used their intelligence to develop tools and technology. Although their tools were still made of stone, they now had specialized items such as chisels and borers. They made these tools by chipping small flakes off carefully selected cores, or lumps, of flint. To chip off a flake of the right size and sharpness, a Neanderthal flintworker needed skill, patience, and a very great deal of practice.

Some of the most fascinating evidence about the Neanderthals comes from their burial sites. Several of these have been discovered, from the Dordogne, France, to the Zagros Mountains in Iran. They reveal the bodies placed carefully in their graves. Items such as animal horns or bones were deliberately placed around them, probably as part of a burial ritual. Sites like these have led modern archaeologists to believe that the Neanderthals were the first hominids to develop burial ceremonies. The burial sites also provided a great deal of evidence that enabled scientists to work out what these people looked like, from

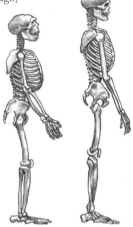

Neanderthal   Modern human

◄ SKELETONS
Stockily built and with a large head, Neanderthals were strong hominids with brains about as big as our own. Modern humans were taller and more upright.

NEANDERTHAL LIFE
During much of the Neanderthals' lifetime, Europe and Asia were in the grip of an ice age. The Neanderthals had to adapt to the cold, making clothes from skins and finding whatever shelter they could. This necessity, together with their large brains, made them inventive and adaptable.

chopper

scraper

borer

◄ NEANDERTHAL TOOLS
The Neanderthals developed different tools for scraping, cutting, butchering, and boring holes in hides. These flint-working skills have been perfected over many generations.

◄ POLLEN GRAINS
By examining prehistoric pollen under a microscope, scientists have found that trees such as alder, birch, oak, and elm grew in areas in which the Neanderthals lived.

▲ NEANDERTHAL GRAVE
Skeletons from this grave at La Chapelle-aux-Saints in France, were found to be deformed and stooping. This could mean the people suffered from arthritis.

flower offerings

bone offerings

animal horns

◀ BURIAL
A group of Neanderthals buries one of their dead. As mourners look on, two members of the group make offerings of pollen and flowers, which are placed carefully on and around the deceased's body. Animal horns are positioned to mark the grave. Rituals like this are the earliest known ceremonies.

their stocky build to the size of their heads and brains.

Some of the skeletons showed signs of bone diseases, such as arthritis, that must have developed over many years. Any individual who developed such a disease would not have been able to hunt and gather food. Other members of their family group must have fed them and looked after them. So besides being intelligent, the Neanderthals may have been the first carers, helping relatives who were not able to fend for themselves. The Neanderthals died out around 35,000 years ago, but it is not certain why. They may have perished through disease or have been killed by Cro-Magnons, *Homo sapiens* who lived at the same time. New evidence is now being found to suggest that Neanderthals interbred with Cro-Magnon people.

▲ NEANDERTHAL SITES
The homeland of the Neanderthals stretched from France and Germany to Mesopotamia in the east. The eastern and western populations were separated during ice ages, but both groups produced similar tools and buried their dead in a similar way.

Key Dates

- 120,000 B.C. Neanderthals living from Europe to Mesopotamia.

- 100,000–40,000 B.C. Neanderthals develop stone tools for several different purposes.

- 100,000 B.C. Neanderthals and *Homo sapiens* both living at Qafzeh, Israel.

- 50,000 B.C. Remains of a burial site of this date found at Shanidar Cave, northern Iraq.

- 40,000 B.C. Skull of this date found at Monte Circeo, Italy, had been smashed to remove the brain.

- 35,000 B.C. Neanderthals die out.

Wise Man

▲ FIRE
The discovery of fire by Homo erectus *was an enormous technological advance that* Homo sapiens *would have inherited.*

Y THE TIME OF THE Neanderthals, members of our own species, *Homo sapiens,* or "wise man," were also living in many parts of the world. In some places, Neanderthals and humans lived close together, which suggests that Neanderthals could not have been our direct ancestors. If they lived together, we could not have evolved from both species. If this is correct, who were they?

Homo sapiens may have evolved from *Homo erectus,* or from another similar hominid that has not yet been discovered. Hominid bones, found in sites all over the world, seem to share features of *Homo erectus* and *Homo sapiens.* Although similar in size to ourselves, these hominids have bone ridges above the eyes and flattened skulls rather than dome-like heads. They date mostly from around 150,000 to 120,000 years ago and are classified by archaeologists as archaic *Homo sapiens.*

Some remains of *Homo sapiens* date from not long after these "archaic" bones.

◀ HUMAN FORM
The first members of Homo sapiens *were similar in appearance to modern people, except that they were generally somehat shorter. Their upright build made them well adapted to walking on two legs.*

▶ COUNTING STICK
Lengths of bone with small notches cut into them have been found at some Homo sapiens *sites. These may have been counting devices or an early form of writing. They may have been used to record a person's share of food.*

◀ EARLY HUMAN SKULL
Early humans had broad skulls that contained large brains. Their faces were flat, so they did not have the ape-like appearance of hominids like Homo habilis *or the Neanderthals.*

THE EARLY HUNTERS

The search for food was the most important part of life for early *Homo sapiens.* Some groups hunted herds of antelopes on the grasslands. Others went into the hills after wild sheep and goats or to the coast in search of seals and seafood.

◀ SEALS
For northern people who lived near the sea, animals such as seals were a valuable quarry. The animals provided a supply of meat, skins, bones (for tool-making), and blubber.

▲ BONE CARVING
Among the hominids, humans are the only artists. Early hunters liked to carve the creatures they chased, and animal bone was an ideal material—soft enough to carve but hard enough to last.

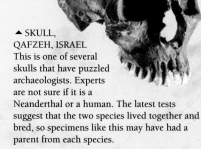

▲ SKULL, QAFZEH, ISRAEL
This is one of several skulls that have puzzled archaeologists. Experts are not sure if it is a Neanderthal or a human. The latest tests suggest that the two species lived together and bred, so specimens like this may have had a parent from each species.

Some experts think humans evolved in one area of Africa and then spread gradually across the world. This idea, which archaeologists refer to as the "Out of Africa" theory, is backed up by research based on DNA. This is the chemical in *Homo sapiens* bodies containing genes.

Other scientists believe that modern humans evolved separately in different parts of the world. For example, the population in Southeast Asia could have descended from *Homo erectus* people on Java. Europeans could have evolved from hominids from the Middle East that had interbred with Neanderthals.

By 100,000 to 90,000 years ago, modern humans had evolved in southern and eastern Africa. From here they traveled northward, crossing the Sahara and reaching the Middle East. For thousands of years the Sahara was wetter than it is today, and it was covered with grasslands cropped by grazing mammals. Hominids could cross this green Sahara with ease. By 75,000 years ago there were modern humans in eastern Asia. Later still, they would reach and settle in Europe.

As our ancestors spread across the globe, they settled in many different environments, from the warm African grasslands to the cold forests of northern Europe. They used their skills to adapt to each new place, using local materials to make clothes and huts, finding out about plants and animals, and learning how to fish. These early people were very advanced compared to many species.

▶ PREPARING SKINS

A hunted animal was not just a source of meat. The skins of larger creatures were removed, scraped clean, and trimmed. Then they were made into clothes, coverings for shelters, and simple bags and containers.

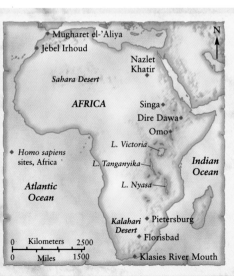

◀ EARLY HUMAN SITES

By 35,000 years ago, early humans had spread across most of Africa. They developed different lifestyles and tools to cope with the different conditions and materials that they found. The people of northern Africa, for example, produced quite finely worked flint scrapers and hand axes, similar to those made by the Neanderthals in Europe. In the south, however, many of the tools were much less finely chipped stone points and scrapers, but they were still sharp and effective.

Key Dates

- 150,000–120,000 B.C. Archaic *Homo sapiens*, the most ancient form of our own species, appears.

- 100,000 B.C. Modern humans begin to evolve in Africa.

- 100,000–70,000 B.C. African sites south of the Sahara show signs of modern human occupation. *Homo erectus* is still alive but is slowly replaced by *Homo sapiens*.

- 100,000–40,000 B.C. The Sahara is cooler than today. Hominids cross it to reach northern Africa.

- 75,000 B.C. Ice sheets in the northern hemisphere begin to get larger.

The First Europeans

▲ BISON CAVE PAINTING
When they discovered how to make colours out of earth and minerals, people began to paint pictures like this bison.

L IFE WAS HARD FOR THE first humans who lived in Europe. The climate was colder than it is today. Food could be difficult to find, and dangerous animals lurked in the forests. People survived by adapting and by becoming skilled at making things, such as tools and shelters. Slowly, over many thousands of years, they perfected the essential skills for survival.

The early Europeans are often called Cro-Magnons, after a site in the Dordogne, France. Cro-Magnon people kept themselves warm by making clothes from animal skins. They sheltered in caves when they could, but natural shelter was not always easy to find. They learned how to make simple homes, using whatever materials they could find. Tree branches provided a framework; this was covered with turf or animal skins to keep out the wind and rain. Another solution was to make a framework from the massive bones of woolly mammoths they had killed.

The Cro-Magnons were skilled toolmakers. Their best and sharpest tools were made from flint, which they could work into small points for spearheads and knives. They also used materials such as bone and deer antler to make tools. Small pieces of bone could be carved to make pointed needles, and antlers could be adapted to make tools such as hammers.

Wood was another useful material. Small flakes of flint could be wedged into a twig to make a knife with a handle. The shafts of spears were also made of wood. It is likely that wood was used in many other ways too, such as making simple containers, but all evidence of this has perished with time.

The greatest achievement of the early European people was in their art. It ranged from sculpture to cave painting and tells us a great deal about everyday life. Pictures of

◄ KALEMBA ROCK SHELTER
About 35,000 years ago, hunter-gatherers used this natural shelter at Kalemba in Zambia. Like other similar shelters all over Africa, it provided a good resting place for people out hunting animals or searching for plants to eat.

GROWING SKILLS

The remains and tools of early *Homo sapiens* seem primitive, but early humans were in fact very intelligent. They were using their abilities to adapt to all sorts of different environments. Human language must also have been developing during this period, but unfortunately no record of it exists.

◄ BEZOAR GOAT
This species of goat was a popular quarry for hunters in the rocky, mountainous regions of the Middle East. Groups of hunters would drive a herd into a canyon. Then they could kill as many as they needed and share out the meat among a large number of people.

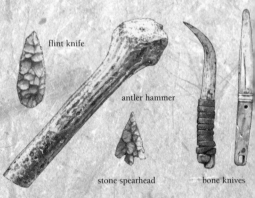

flint knife

antler hammer

stone spearhead

bone knives

▲ TOOLS
People learned to use several different materials to make tools. If no good stone was available, people used bone and antler for knives and points, as well as for tools like hammers.

◀ HUNTERS' CAMP
Early hunters traveled quite long distances looking for food but returned to regular camps at places where there was shelter and a water supply. A campsite could be used by members of the same tribe or group for thousands of years.

animals show the creatures they hunted, from wild oxen and deer to woolly mammoths and rhinoceroses. It is also possible to make out the skin clothing they wore. Female figurines suggest that the people worshiped a mother goddess or goddess of fertility. People who were intelligent enough to produce the art and tools of the early Europeans probably also had quite an advanced society. Although they lived in family-based bands, it is quite likely that these small groups may have come together at certain times. They probably joined together to hunt or for religious ceremonies celebrating important times of the year.

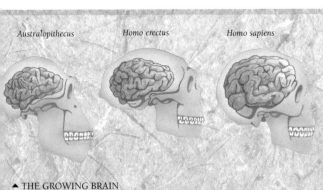

Australopithecus   *Homo erectus*   *Homo sapiens*

▲ THE GROWING BRAIN
Studies of early *Homo sapiens* show that their brains were similar in size to those of modern humans and much bigger than those of the earlier hominids. The australopithecines, which were the size of modern chimpanzees, had brains with an average cubic capacity just over half that of *Homo erectus*. Even the brain of *Homo erectus* was little over half the total volume of *Homo sapiens'* brain. Human inventiveness, creativity, language, and social skills are all the result of our bigger brains.

Key Dates

- 43,000 B.C. *Homo sapiens* established in Bulgaria.

- 40,000 B.C. Humans in western Europe living alongside Neanderthals.

- 35,000 B.C. The Neanderthals die out. *Homo sapiens* is the only human form in Europe.

- 20,000 B.C. French and Spanish flint-workers find out how to bake flints so they can be pressure flaked to make very fine shapes.

- 16,000–12,000 B.C. Human settlement in Russia and Siberia. Mammoth-bone huts built at Mezhrich.

- 6000 B.C. Europeans develop microliths, tools made of tiny fragments of flint.

The Ice Age

▲ CARVING
This head is carved from a piece of mammoth tusk, a favorite material for sculpture during the Ice Age.

THE EARTH'S WEATHER IS ALWAYS changing. For the last two million years, the temperature of the planet has seesawed up and down. This has produced a series of warm periods with cold ice ages in between. The last of these ice ages reached its peak about 18,000 B.C. The time around this peak (30,000 to 12,000 B.C.) is so important in human history that it is always known as the Ice Age.

Humans had spread over much of the world by the beginning of the most recent Ice Age. All that time, the ice sheets had pushed down from the north, covering huge areas of the globe. Places such as Scandinavia, Siberia, and northern Britain became unfit for humans.

During this period, much of northern Europe was covered with sparse tundra. Large parts of Spain, Greece, and the Balkans were in forests. The area north of the Black Sea in Russia was a vast grassland. These varied habitats were a challenge to early people, and they had to adapt to different conditions. Big-game hunters moved across the Russian plains. Hunter-fishers lived on the tundra and at the edge of the ice sheets. Hunters and food gatherers took shelter in the forests. People had to devise different tools, hunting techniques and social skills to suit these varied lifestyles.

Ice Age tools are more varied than those of previous peoples. People in the Ice Age still used stone for their knives and choppers. But they used more bone and

◀ MAMMOTH
This large Ice Age mammal ranged widely across Europe, Asia, and North America. It died out around 10,000 years ago.

ICE AGE LIFE

The Ice Age made life difficult in many places. The cold was not just uncomfortable, it meant that some food plants could not survive. In addition, many areas had few or no trees, so that people had no wood to make shelters. These difficulties forced people to find new ways of life. They had to experiment with new foods (such as fish) and new materials (such as, bones and antlers).

▼ MAKING FIRE
In a cold, damp climate, fire became even more important as a source of warmth. Making fire by rubbing sticks together to create a spark may have spread across Europe during the Ice Age.

◀ REINDEER
There are many surviving tools, harpoons, and carvings made from antler. This shows that reindeer-like animals were hunted across Europe during the Ice Age. Reindeer provided tasty, nutritious meat, as well as hides, bone, and antler.

▲ HARPOON POINTS
Ice Age hunters used harpoons for killing animals such as seals and for fishing in the rivers for salmon. The points took a long time to carve from deer antler and were prized possessions.

▶ MAMMOTH HUNTING

Large, fierce, and with two powerful tusks, woolly mammoths were an awesome sight for the people of the Ice Age. But these dangerous creatures were such a good source of meat, skins, bones, and ivory that the people risked injury or even death hunting and trapping them.

antler than before. They discovered how to use antler to make strong handles for stone blades and ax heads. They carved bone to make needles, which were essential to sew together hides and furs for warm clothes.

People still hunted large mammals such as the woolly mammoth. They also learned how to track and hunt animals that live in herds, such as reindeer. This gave them a rich source of hides, meat, and antlers.

Because resources were scarce, Ice Age people probably became the first traders, swapping food and materials. Flints and furs, for example, could be traded for food in times of shortage. People traveled more, they met other groups, and they probably found out about new sources of food. Contact with other tribes was an aid to survival. When different groups met, it became necessary to have a leader to act as spokesman. This was also a time when personal adornment first became important. A bone pendant or bright body paint could mark out the leader of a group.

▲ ICE AGE WORLD
Lower sea levels made the world's continents larger during the Ice Age, and some landmasses that are now separate were joined together. But the ice sheets in Europe, Asia, and the Americas made vast areas of this land unfit for human life.

Key Dates

- 32,000–28,000 B.C. Aurignacian culture in western Europe produces flint scrapers and sharpened blades.

- 30,000–12,000 B.C. Main period of last Ice Age.

- 24,000 B.C. Hunter-gatherers in Europe build permanent dwellings.

- 20,000 B.C. Hunters in western Europe develop spears and spear-throwers. Hunters in Poland use mammoth-tusk boomerangs.

- 18,000 B.C. Peak of Ice Age.

- 18,000–12,500 B.C. People settled near Kebara Cave, Israel, make grinding stones. This suggests they were gathering and processing grains.

Images of the Ice Age

THE PREHISTORIC CAVE paintings of Europe show a wide variety of creatures. These include groups of wild horses, herds of reindeer and wild oxen, wild cats, birds, and mammoths. The animals are shown in action, galloping and running across the cave walls as if they are being chased by human hunters. They are dramatic action pictures, yet they were produced in dark, damp conditions in chilly caves. Ice Age artists also made sculptures and modeled figures from clay. They engraved cave walls and carved antlers and mammoth tusks into models of animals.

The paintings and sculptures are often hidden so deep in underground caverns that many of them were not rediscovered until the 1900s. It is not known why the paintings were hidden away like this. In fact, no one really knows why the pictures were produced at all. Most experts agree that there was probably some religious reason for the paintings. They may have been used in magic ceremonies designed to help hunters or to promote fertility. Sometimes there are several different outlines in the same place, one drawn over another. This makes some cave paintings and engravings very difficult to see. Experts have spent many hours redrawing them in

▲ MAMMOTH CARVING
Ice Age art was not always realistic, and carvers often made striking, stylized shapes. In the case of this mammoth, the shape of the animal reflects the shape of the bone from which it is carved.

▲ PAINTING TECHNIQUES
Artists used brushes or pads of animal hair when painting on cave walls. They sometimes put on the paint with their fingers or created a bold outline by drawing with charcoal.

ICE AGE ART

Because we do not know why Ice Age artists made their pictures and sculptures, it is difficult to decide what their work means. It does show how important animals and the natural world were to them. The cave paintings show the kind of animals these people ate and hunted and also which creatures they thought were the most powerful. These images, and the small carvings of the time, also provide some clues about Ice Age beliefs.

◀ ANTLER SPEAR-THROWER
A spear-thrower helped a hunter hurl his spear faster and farther than he otherwise could by acting as an extension of his arm. This made it easier to kill swift creatures such as deer. Hunters prized their spear-throwers, which were usually made of antler. This material lent itself to carving, and spear-throwers are often beautifully decorated. Swift-running animals like the horse shown here were favorite subjects.

◀ VENUS FIGURINE
Carvings of female figures, with their hips and bellies enlarged, have often been found at Ice Age sites. Archaeologists think they are fertility goddesses, and so have named them "Venus" figures, after the Roman goddess of love.

▶ IVORY HEAD
This female head from France, carved in ivory, shows a goddess. Goddess figures have been found in most areas of Europe, from France to Russia, so goddesses were probably the most important deities in Ice Age religion.

their notebooks to try to make the outlines clearer. For the prehistoric artist, the act of making the image seems to have been more important than the finished result. Perhaps the actual process of painting or engraving was part of a religious ceremony.

Ice Age painters used chalk to make white, charcoal for black, ocher (a kind of earth) for yellow, and iron oxide for red. Sometimes artists used minerals that they could heat to make other colors. The pigments were mixed with water and applied with fur pads, animal-hair brushes, or just with the artist's fingers.

Another technique involved spitting the paint out of the mouth or a reed to make a simple spray effect. The artists used oil lamps to light the caves and sometimes built crude wooden frameworks to gain extra height while working. With these simple techniques, Ice Age artists produced images that were surprisingly complex for such a simple society.

▲ CAVE PAINTING, LASCAUX
The caves at Lascaux, France, contain perhaps the most brilliant of all the known prehistoric paintings. Discovered in 1940, they show a variety of animals, including reindeer and horses. These finely drawn, brightly colored paintings began to show signs of damage in the 1960s because the atmosphere in the caves was affected by so many visitors. The caves were closed to the public, who now visit a replica called Lascaux II.

◀ ANTELOPE
This painting from a cave at Font de Gaume, France, shows the skill of the ancient artists. They caught the outline of the creature's head and horns, and cleverly shaded the animal's hide to create a sense of its bulk.

▶ MAKING PAINT
Artists found their colors in the earth and rocks. They mixed soils and minerals that they found with a medium such as water or animal fat. This produced a type of spreadable paint. They could also draw directly onto the rock surface with pieces of charcoal (burnt wood) or chalk.

iron oxide

brushstrokes   chalk   charcoal

◀ LAMP
Many cave paintings are hidden in dark, underground caverns. The artists needed light to see what they were doing, so they used fires, flaming torches, or stone lamps like this one. The animal fat was burned in the lamps, to give a bright, but rather smelly, flame. Several hundred Ice Age lamps have been found by archaeologists.

Key Dates

- 30,000B.C. Earliest European cave art.
- 30,000B.C. European musicians make flutes from lengths of animal bone.
- 23,000B.C. First cave paintings made in the Dordogne, France.
- 23,000B.C. Venus figurines made in France and central Europe.
- 18,000–8000B.C. Main period of cave painting in caves at Lascaux, France, and Altamira, Spain.
- 16,000B.C. Antler and bone carving reaches its peak. Finely engraved and carved spear points and spear-throwers made.
- 11,000B.C. Cave painting ends.

The First Australians

▲ ENGRAVINGS
These patterns were cut into rocks at Panaramitee, Australia, thousands of years ago. They may be the world's oldest rock engravings.

D URING THE ICE AGE, the sea level was much lower than it is today. The channels separating Australia from islands such as Timor in Indonesia were far narrower. As a result, groups of islanders took to the sea in bamboo rafts or simple boats in search of fish and shellfish. Some time before 32,000 years ago some Indonesians found themselves on the coast of what is now Australia. No one knows whether they had deliberately looked for new land were blown off-course on one of their fishing trips. They moved inland and became the first humans to inhabit the Australian continent.

The remains of early settlement in Australia are quite patchy. The people were spread over a wide area and must have covered vast distances both by sea and on foot. Stone tools, hearths, shell debris, fish bones, and other remnants point to a scattered population between 32,000 and 24,000 years ago. Important sites include Devil's Lair Cave near Perth, Western Australia, a rock shelter near the Cleland Hills in Northern Territory, and Koonalda Cave in South Australia.

At Devil's Lair, archaeologists found several items that were probably used in religious ceremonies. There were some stone plaques and a pit with human teeth that had been removed by sharp blows. At Koonalda Cave, the inhabitants engraved lines on the rock walls. Native Australians carried on making rock engravings into the 1900s. The finds dating from prehistoric times show how far back a rich native Australian culture goes.

Many early Australian sites were occupied for thousands of years. This can also make exact

▶ DUGOUT CANOE
Early sailors, like the people who first crossed from Southeast Asia to Australia, may have hollowed out and smoothed wooden logs to make simple dugout canoes.

A SCATTERED PEOPLE
The first Australians traveled vast distances across their country to find food and good campsites. When they settled, they spread out thinly across the country. Sites in the south, which were well away from their original landing places, seem to have been most popular. The settlement process probably took place very slowly, spreading across the country over thousands of years.

◀ NECKLACE
People wore necklaces made of shells and animal teeth. Jewelry like this may have been a sign that the wearer was an important person. Such necklaces have been found in Asia as well as Australia. This indicates that the two regions were linked by a common people.

◀ HAND STENCILS
Stencils like this were probably made by spitting paint around and over the artist's hand. This type of art has been practiced in Australia since at least 22,000 B.C. The images, which are on the walls of rock shelters in southern and eastern Australia, show the importance of art to the island continent's earliest people.

dating of the art and artifacts difficult for archaeologists. One rock shelter, at Puritjarra, was used for nearly 7,000 years.

People had reached the island of Tasmania at the southeast tip of Australia by 32,000 years ago. They remained there even when the final Ice Age was at its coldest, when much of the island was covered by tundra and grassland. They lived in caves and rock shelters and survived by hunting the local animals, mainly the kangaroo and the wallaby. The new Tasmanians developed their own style of art. They painted hand stencils on cave walls and made tools

from a natural form of glass that they discovered in a crater formed by a meteorite from space.

The native people of Australia developed a lifestyle long ago that has lasted in some places to the present day. Over the millennia they adapted as their environment changed, from the chill Ice Age to the hot, dry climate of today.

▼ MAKING TOOLS
Early Australians became expert stoneworkers. They could chip away stones to make tools that were the right shape for the job and grind the edges of tools such as axes to make them sharp. Some of their tools were traded over long distances.

◀ EXPLORERS' MAP
Because the sea level was lower, larger pieces of land were above water, so the first people to travel to Australia had a shorter sea journey than travelers would have to make today. They probably crossed from places such as Java or the Celebes, sailing from island to island until they reached the northwestern coast of Australia. Even for such short trips, they needed to be good sailors and navigators. They probably built up their sailing skills over many years fishing off the Southeast Asian coasts.

Key Dates

- 30,000B.C. Human settlement of Australia probably begins.

- 29,000B.C. People are living in Tasmania, which is linked to the Australian mainland by a land bridge.

- 25,000B.C. Puritjarra Rock Shelter, near the Cleland Hills, Northern Territory, is occupied.

- 24,000B.C. Signs of human occupation near Lake Mungo, New South Wales.

- 22,000B.C. Traces of human settlement at Koonalda Cave, on the Nullaboor Plain, South Australia.

- 10,000B.C. The population of native Australians is about 300,000 people.

Early Americans

THE FIRST AMERICANS probably came from the extreme north tip of Asia, which is now Siberia. In the Ice Age the two continents were connected by a land bridge. The first peoples to cross this narrow neck of land found themselves in North America's bleakest, coldest spot. There would have been little vegetation. Most of their food came from hunting and fishing. They were well prepared for this, because the climate in Siberia was similar to that in North America. Many moved south in search of better weather and more plentiful food.

Archaeologists disagree about exactly when the first Americans arrived. The earliest firm evidence of

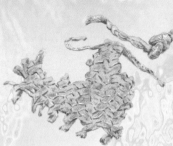

▲ THE JOURNEY FROM SIBERIA
It was a long, hard journey from Siberia across the land bridge to North America. We do not know what made people start this journey, but perhaps the harsh Ice Age conditions made them want to look for a place where food, warmth, and comfort were easier to find.

humans dates to between 15,000 and 12,000 years ago. However, in the same period, there is more widespread evidence for a hunting people who lived in western North America. Archeologists call them the

THE GREAT MIGRATION

How do we know that the first Americans came from Siberia? One clue lies in the way the early Americans made tools and weapons. Many chipped tiny flint blades from bigger lumps of stone. They jammed these flints into grooves along the edge of a piece of bone to make a spearhead. Spearheads with this design have been found in both Siberia and North America.

▲ CLOVIS POINTS
North American mammoth hunters fitted these finely worked sharp stone points to their spears. They made these points out of several different types of stone.

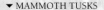

▼ MAMMOTH TUSKS
These fossilized tusks are among many mammoth remains preserved at the Hot Springs mammoth site, South Dakota. They show that the first American hunters were catching the same quarry as their ancestors in Asia.

▲ WEAVING
A few fragments of twine have survived at Guitarrero Cave, Peru, to show that people could weave 10,000 years ago. These pieces may have been part of a bag or similar container.

Clovis people. They left behind finely worked flint spearheads, now called Clovis points after the town in New Mexico where the tools were found. These have been found at several places near the bones of large mammals such as mammoth and buffalo.. Clovis people probably hunted solitary animals, driving them into swamps where they could be killed.

As the ice melted, the mammoths became extinct, although no one really knows why. The Clovis people vanished as a variety of new environments, from vast woodlands to arid deserts, developed in North America. People learned to adapt to each environment, evolving into distinct societies, whose lifestyles changed little until recent centuries.

In South America there is also evidence for human settlement by 12,000 years ago. At Monte Verde, Chile, the cremated remains of humans have been found in a cave. This site also contains remains of two rows of huts with wooden frames that supported a covering of animal skins. The huts had clay-lined pits for cooking, and there were larger, communal hearths outside.

It is just possible that human life began in South America much earlier than the

▶ MONTE VERDE
The huts at Monte Verde, Chile, made of wood covered with skins, provide the earliest evidence in America for manmade shelters. The remains were preserved in peaty soil, along with items such as a wooden bowl and digging sticks.

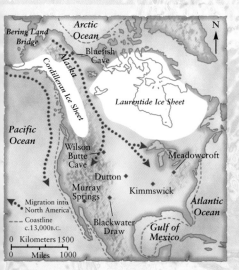

◀ SPEARHEAD
Spears, with notched bone spearheads bound tightly to wooden shafts with animal sinews, were used by early American hunters.

huts at Monte Verde. At Pedra Furada Rock Shelter, Brazil, there are areas of painted rock which some scientists date to around 32,000 years ago. Not all authorities agree with this dating, or with similar dates for some of the stone tools found at Monte Verde. If the early dates are correct, it is likely that settlement also began much earlier in North America but that the people left no surviving remains.

◀ NEW ARRIVALS
The first North Americans worked their way between the two main ice sheets. The Bering Land Bridge was created between Siberia and Alaska because the sea level was some 330 feet lower than it is today. Some people may also have come along the west coast on boats or rafts, stopping every so often along the edge of the Cordilleran Ice Sheet. When they finally reached beyond the ice, they found a vast empty land. Some people quickly moved east and west, while others pushed on further south.

Key Dates

- 13,000 B.C. Hunters from Siberia cross the Bering Land Bridge.

- 12,500 B.C. Humans at Meadowcroft Rock Shelter, Pittsburgh, Pennsylvania—the earliest known settlement in North America.

- 11,000 B.C. People living at Monte Verde in southern Chile.

- 9000 B.C. Clovis people hunting on the Great Plains.

- 8000 B.C. Human settlers are accompanied by dogs.

- 7500 B.C. The people of the Sloan site, Arkansas, bury their dead. This cemetery is the earliest discovered in North America.

The Thaw Begins

FISH CARVING
Stone carvings of fishes, like this one, were found at Lepenski Vir on the river Danube. They may have portrayed a fish god.

At the end of the Ice Age there was a great change in the world's climate. In much of Europe, Asia, and North America, the ice melted, making the sea level rise and causing floods in flat areas near the sea. The land bridge between Siberia and Alaska disappeared, cutting off North America from Asia. Britain, which had been joined to Europe, was now cut off by the North Sea. Large areas of land were lost around the coasts of Denmark and Sweden.

The change must have been terrifying at first. Many people fled the floods to settle in new areas. Their way of life changed. At the same time, the warmer weather transformed the landscape. In many places, ice and tundra were

THATCHED TENTS
The Middle Stone Age settlement of Lepenski Vir was home to around 100 hunting and fishing people. They lived in tent-like houses made of wooden poles which were probably covered with thatch.

replaced by thick woods of birch and mixed forests in northern Europe, and deciduous woods in the south. People soon realized that these changes gave them new types of food. Among the woods lived animals such as wild pig and deer. Near the coast there were seals, waterfowl, and, in many places, shellfish. Food was more plentiful because the climate was warmer.

People developed new methods of hunting and fishing. These new techniques were more efficient than previous methods, so they did not have to move around so much to hunt for food. They set up special camps where food of a certain type was plentiful, or where they could mine flint to make their tools and weapons.

Most settlements in this period were by rivers or near the sea, where the people could usually rely on a good food supply. Rivers and coastal waters were the highways of the Stone Age. Rivers provided a way of traveling through the dense forests. People paddled along in their dugout canoes, perhaps exchanging valuable goods, such as furs or flint tools, with other travelers they met along the way.

LIFE DURING THE THAW

As the ice melted, some people moved inland, but for many the sea was too useful to leave behind. Such shellfish as oysters and whelks supplied tasty, nourishing food, so many people returned to the coast for at least part of the year.

scrapers, blades, and points from Star Carr

FOREST FRUITS
The trees and shrubs of the new woodlands and forest edges yielded fruits such as blackberries to feed European gatherers.

WILD BOAR
This woodland animal thrived in Europe after the thaw. It became a favorite target for many European hunters.

TOOLS FROM STAR CARR
Hunter-gatherers camped regularly at Star Carr, near a lake in Yorkshire, England, at the end of the final Ice Age. They left behind many stone tools, such as scrapers, which they must have used to prepare animal skins, and smaller sharp cutting blades for butchering meat.

The new lifestyle meant that the people who lived in Europe after the Ice Age were on the whole better fed and more comfortable than their ancestors. They were more settled, so they had time to develop more advanced toolmaking skills. This made them more successful still. As a result, many more of their children began to survive to become adults. The total number of people began to rise, and the population began to spread, finding better places to settle and new sources of food.

▼ PINCEVANT

These round tents, held up with wooden poles, were the summer homes of people at Pincevant, France, at the end of the final Ice Age. All that was left to show modern archaeologists that tents had been pitched there were the rings of stones that had held the edges in place, together with hearths and some animal bones.

Spread of broadleaved forest
- up to 11,000 B.C.
- 11,000-8,500 B.C.
- 8,500-7,500 B.C.
- 7,500-5,000 B.C.

Scandinavia

EUROPE

Atlantic Ocean

Mediterranean Sea

AFRICA

N

0 Kilometers 800
0 Miles 500

◀ SPREADING FORESTS
As the ice melted, forests spread slowly across Europe, covering the area in broadleaved trees. The spread of the forests began in the south, working its way north over a period of about 6,000 years toward Poland and Scandinavia, where mixed conifer and broadleaved forests grew. This new pattern of forests and woodland provided large areas of Europe with their typical landscape, one that survived for thousands of years. It still survives in some parts of Germany, central Europe, and Scandinavia.

Key Dates

- 13,000 B.C. The ice thaws, sea levels rise, and lowland areas flood.

- 11,000 B.C. The dog is domesticated in the Middle East.

- 8000 B.C. Temperatures reach roughly their present levels in Europe.

- 8000 B.C. The Mesolithic period, or Middle Stone Age, begins in Europe.

- 7500 B.C. Red deer hunters settle at Star Carr, Yorkshire, England.

- 6500 B.C. Britain is cut off from Europe.

- 5500 B.C. Denmark is cut off from the rest of Scandinavia.

- 5000 B.C. Deciduous forests cover much of Europe.

A Better Food Supply

▲ MATTOCK HEAD
Deer antler was a good material to make a heavy tool such as a mattock. This was used by gatherers for loosening soil and cutting away plant roots for food.

MANY THINGS CHANGED IN North America at the end of the Ice Age. People were suddenly much freer to go where they wanted in search of food and raw materials. They found a range of different regions, from the grassy Great Plains to the drier areas of the southwest, all of which could be settled. At first they moved south, following the mammals and hunting them with their stone-pointed spears. They also spread out east and west across the continent, finding more and better sources of flint for tools and weapons. Archaeologists have traced many of the stone tools to where they were first made. Some of them were carried hundreds, or even thousands, of miles, which shows how far the hunters journeyed.

It took several thousand years for the climate and vegetation to settle down into the pattern that still exists today. As this happened, species such as mammoths became extinct, and people turned to smaller animals for food. The hunters also developed lighter, more accurate spears, which enables them to bring down game without having to ambush it first. On the grasslands there were still large creatures, such as buffalo. These provided hunters with a number of different products, such as meat to eat and hides to make leather and bones for tools. From around 9000 B.C., the people of the plains began to develop a lifestyle that would continue, with very little change, for many thousands of years.

The people of Asia, like the Europeans, took advantage of a better, more reliable food supply. They were healthier, and their population began to increase. However, they still relied on many of their old techniques for survival and shelter. In some places, people started to settle down and build permanent huts. Elsewhere, hunters still built temporary shelters from branches or mammoth bones and hides.

As the ice thawed in Africa and the Middle East, many areas

◀ ANTLER HEADDRESS
Archaeologists found this unusual antler headdress at the British Stone Age site of Star Carr, Yorkshire. It may have been used in a religious ceremony or as a disguise when hunting deer.

HUNTERS' WEAPONS

By the late Ice Age, weapons had improved. Although spearheads and harpoon points were still made of stone, antler, and bone, they were carefully carved so they worked well whenever they were used. When food was scarce, a hunter could not afford to lose his quarry because a blunt spear allowed an animal to escape.

▶ ANTLER POINTS
Hunters used deer antler to make deadly harpoon points. By carving away notches along one edge, then sharpening one or both ends, they made a barbed point. The advantage of this was that when a weapon was thrown at an animal it went in easily, but would not slip out as the creature ran away. Barbed points are still used by Arctic hunters.

◀ REPAIRING SPEARS
Stone spearheads such as North American Clovis points are virtually everlasting. But wooden spear shafts often break or split, so hunters had to fit their points to new ones. They fixed the points by splitting the shaft, jamming in the head, and binding animal sinew around the joint.

▼ HOME OF SKIN AND BONE

Like the people of the Ukraine, Siberian hunters built homes out of large animal bones and tusks, covered with skins and reinforced with timber if they could find it. Stones weighted down the skins on the ground. The people may have learned how to build these tents in the Ukraine before traveling eastward to their new homes.

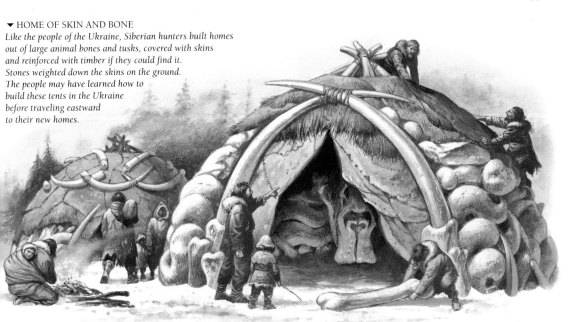

that had been desert were covered with vegetation. Plants began to flourish in the Nile Valley and the eastern Mediterranean. This was a land of wild grasses, and people began to gather their seeds, grind them into flour, and make bread to eat. One group of people who we know did this were the Natufians, a people who lived near the Wadi en-Natuf, in what is now Israel.

These cereal gatherers were learning a lot of vital information about the various kinds of grain. For example, which provided the tastiest seeds, when best to harvest them, and the most effective tools to use. Later, they would put this knowledge to good use, changing to a settled way of life and becoming some of the world's first farmers.

Removing flakes from the flint.

Carefully shaping the edge. The hand is protected by animal skin.

Putting the point into the cleft stick.

◄ MAKING A POINT
A hunter hit a lump of flint with an antler hammer, removing bits from either side until the piece was the right thickness and shape. Then he took a pointed piece of antler and worked around the edge of the point, removing chips to produce a razor-sharp edge. Next he put the point in a cleft stick and wrapped it around with sinews to protect it. He then hit the base of the point with his hammer, to remove a flake and make a fluted shape to fit the shaft.

Key Dates

- 10,000 B.C. The Natufian culture develops in western Asia. Its people build round stone huts, herd goats, and gather wild emmer wheat.

- 9000 B.C. Population levels begin to rise in Asia, encouraging people to take up new lifestyles such as herding.

- 9000 B.C. People in the Americas begin to hunt a wider range of smaller mammals. A more settled lifestyle begins to evolve.

- 5000 B.C. Tools in America become more specialized, and grindstones are created for processing plant foods.

- 3500 B.C. People in North America begin to live in permanent villages.

Rock Paintings

SAN HUNTERS
This modern rock painting by the San people, or bushmen, from the Kalahari Desert shows hunters chasing their quarry. It is one of many recent rock paintings done in a style similar to that used in prehistoric times.

UNLIKE CAVE PAINTINGS, which were hidden deep underground, rock paintings were made on rocks and cliff faces out in the open air. Some of these drawings are engraved into the rock with a sharp stone tool. Others are painted with natural pigments in a similar way to that used for the cave paintings of the final Ice Age. Rock art occurs all over the world, from Africa to Australia. The drawings are usually easier to find than the cave paintings of western Europe, and in some places they are quite common. Some rock drawings date from 8000B.C., but others were made as recently as the 1800s. The more recent pictures are often similar in style to the ancient images. This makes them difficult to date, but it also shows how the art and lifestyles of many peoples altered little until the early 1900s. Rock art can tell us a great deal about the people who created it—especially the creatures they hunted and farmed, because animals appear in these paintings more than any other subject.

Some of the most interesting and best preserved rock art is found in Africa. In the Saharan region, the types of animals in the pictures show how different the area was compared with the desert of today. After the final Ice Age, when the Sahara was covered in grasslands and dotted with oases

◀ HAND PAINTING
One method used by rock artists was to take some paint into the mouth and spit it onto the rock to produce a stencil of the hand.

THE VARIETY OF ROCK ART

The most common subjects in rock art are animals, people, and patterns. Although the subjects are similar, the style of the pictures can vary greatly around the world. Some, like the paintings of the Sahara, are very realistic. Others, like the human figures of South America, are more like symbols than pictures of real people.

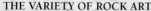

▶ GAZELLES
Artists from the Tassili Massif in the Sahara drew these gazelles. They were painted over 6,000 years ago. This was before the beginning of farming, when Saharan artists were still drawing the animals they hunted for food.

▲ BISON
The people of Bhimbetka, India, made rock drawings of animals for thousands of years. Bison, antelope, and deer, as well as people, were favorite subjects, and some, like this example, were filled in with delicate abstract patterns.

▲ HUMAN FIGURE
This rock engraving of a stylized person comes from Venezuela. No one knows what the circles and curves around it are, but they may be symbols of the Moon or Sun.

or shallow lakes, the area was home to wild oxen and gazelles. The local people hunted these animals and drew them on the walls of their shelters. After about 6000B.C., they began to draw domestic cattle, which shows that the change from hunting to farming near the oases happened around this time.

Other African paintings, such as those of the San people of what is now the Kalahari Desert, show hunters chasing their quarry. They are also shown fishing from their boats and gathering food. Pictures like these are almost certainly more than just decorations on shelter walls. The hunting pictures were probably produced as part of a ceremony performed before the hunt. The people hoped that drawing a successful hunt would make their own hunt turn out well. In a similar way, a picture of a group of men dancing around an antelope was probably intended to transfer some of the real animal's strength to the men of the tribe.

Paintings with a religious or ceremonial purpose are even more common in Australia. Stories of how the world was created have always been important to the native Australians. Each tribe has its own ancestor, usually an animal that is linked with some special part of the landscape. One Australian myth, which tells how the world was made, describes the way in which the rainbow serpent, who came from the sea, slithered onto the shore and created the landscape as he snaked his way inland. Rainbow serpents first begin to appear in rock paintings made by native Australians some 6,000 years ago.

▲ SPIRIT BEINGS
Australian rock painting represents spirits that were believed to be the ancestors of a particular tribe. They formed the center of the tribe's religious beliefs. The ancestors of different groups took different forms. Some were said to be animals; others were features of the landscape. They were all regarded with the deepest reverence by their people, as they are today.

◄ HUNTERS
Many rock drawings were made by hunting peoples, like these figures by the San people of the Kalahari Desert. The painted hunters seem to be moving with great agility, almost like dancers.

▶ LEAF
Depictions of plants are rarer in rock art than animals or people. They do occur occasionally, as in this Australian example from a site in the Northern Territory. Plant pictures may be linked to religion or the ancestors, or may have been done simply to create a decorative effect.

Key Dates

- 25,000B.C. Early inhabitants of Australia may be developing rock art.

- 20,000B.C. Rock artists may already be active in some parts of Africa.

- 11,000B.C. Rock art in central India shows hunters and prey.

- 8500B.C. The earliest rock paintings found in Saharan Africa portray wild animals.

- 8000B.C. The main period of cave painting ends in Europe. Rock art on cliffs and in shallower caves becomes common.

- 6000B.C. Saharan rock artists depict cattle, reflecting the change to the herding of livestock.

The First Farmers

▲ WHEAT
Finding a staple crop that provides basic energy needs is an important step in farming. Wheat is one of the most common. Others are millet, rice and maize.

HUNTERS AND GATHERERS were highly skilled at finding food. However, their success was dependent on the weather, local conditions and luck. If the weather turned bad or the local supplies ran out, people faced starvation. Around 11,000 years ago, a group of people in the Middle East changed this. They began to produce their own food by farming. It was one of the most important developments in the history of humankind.

Farming gave people control over their food supply. They did not have to wander through the countryside looking for food any longer. They could settle in one place, and as a result they began to build stronger, more comfortable houses than before. Farming also offered a more reliable supply of food, although in years when the harvest was bad, people had to return to gathering for a while.

The first farmers lived at the eastern end of the Mediterranean (now Israel, Palestine, and Syria) and in an upland region north of the river Tigris in what now forms parts of Iran and Iraq. This region has more rain than the surrounding plains, and grasses such as wheat and barley grow there naturally. Because of its climate and its shape on the map, the area is now known as the Fertile Crescent.

The people of the Fertile Crescent had gathered wheat seeds for thousands of years. They knew which types grew most vigorously and produced the best grain. By about 9000B.C., they realized that they could plant these grasses and harvest them. At around the same time, they started to herd the wild sheep and goats. These animals provided milk and wool as well as meat. During the next 3,000 years, people also began to keep livestock, pigs, and cattle.

In good years, farming gave the people of the Fertile Crescent more food than they

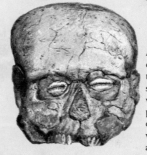

◀ STONE TOWER
Jericho's tallest building was a stone tower. No one knows why the tower was built. It could have been a watchtower, or it might have had some religious purpose.

THE FARMERS' WORLD
Although farming created a lot of hard work, the people of the first agricultural villages did not spend all their time in the fields. In many places, they developed quite complex religious beliefs and ceremonies. They produced new styles of art, including sculptures modeled from plaster and pottery decorated with striking abstract designs of lines and rectangles. They also started to make larger baskets and clay containers for storing surplus grain.

◀ FIGURE SCULPTURE
The world's earliest large-scale human sculptures were produced in Ain Ghazal, Jordan. They were moulded in lime plaster over a skeleton of straw bundles. The eyes were outlined with dark paint. No one knows why they were made.

▶ SPOUTED BOWL
From the early farming site at Khirokitia, Cyprus, came this decorated pottery bowl. It was buried in the grave of an eight-year-old child, and was obviously a favorite object, as it had been repaired before the burial.

◀ PLASTERED SKULL
Around 6000B.C., the religious ceremonies of Jericho involved the use of human skulls. The skulls were covered with plaster, which was molded to copy the person's ears, nose, mouth and other facial features. Cowrie shell were placed in the eye sockets, and teeth were added.

could eat. They stored the surplus in grain bins or baskets and traded it for materials, for tools, or for items such as pots and furniture.

Gradually, the farmers and craftworkers became rich. They built more and bigger houses clustered together. These groups of houses developed into small towns. The houses were made of mud bricks, providing warmth in winter while staying cool in summer. One of the first of these towns was Jericho, built near a spring north of the Dead Sea. The land around the town was good both for growing crops and for grazing herds and flocks of animals, and soon Jericho became a very prosperous town. It was not long before other towns were built in this area.

As farming spread farther afield, it was not very long before other regions began to produce their food in a similar way, and the pattern of human life had changed forever.

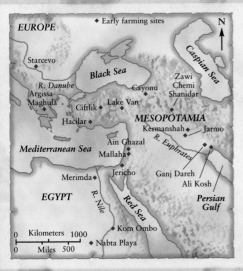

◀ EARLY FARMER
To begin with, farming was difficult, backbreaking work—even more so than the toil of hunting and gathering. There were only stone and wooden hand tools to work the soil. Seed had to be scattered by hand, and harvesting had to be done in the hot sun with a simple stone sickle.

◀ FARMING IN THE FERTILE CRESCENT
To begin with, farming was most successful where there were light soils. These could be easily worked with basic hand tools. There also had to be plants growing wild that were suitable for cultivating. From its beginnings near the Persian Gulf, the river Euphrates and the eastern Mediterranean, farming spread gradually outward. Egypt to the south and Turkey and Greece to the northwest were places where farming arrived early.

Key Dates

- 10,000B.C. Cereal gathering begins in Palestine.

- 9000B.C. Farming begins in the Fertile Crescent.

- 9000B.C. The people of Syria and nearby regions sow wheat.

- 9000B.C. Jericho develops as a small settlement around a spring.

- 8000B.C. Animal herding is well established in the Zagros Mountains.

- 7000B.C. Cereal farming is widespread from Turkey to the Fertile Crescent, in the Zagros Mountains, and in parts of Pakistan.

Plants and Animals

THE FIRST FARMERS DID NOT simply take wild grasses and plant them in rows in their fields. They had to work hard to turn the wild species they found into true cereal crops. To begin with, they had to choose the plants that were the most suitable for food. In Europe and Asia, farmers chose grasses such as wheat and barley. Farmers in eastern Asia grew millet. Tropical African growers cultivated yams. The first farmers in North America selected corn, while those in South America chose potatoes and another root vegetable, manioc.

Farmers watched for the individual plants that were strongest or biggest. American corn farmers, for example, collected the seed from plants yielding the biggest cobs, and sowed these, to produce a crop with larger cobs next year.

Farmers in the Fertile Crescent had a different problem with their wheat. One species that grew well was wild einkorn wheat. But its seeds tended to break off and fall to the ground when they ripened, which made them difficult to harvest. Eventually the farmers noticed that a few plants had seeds that did not fall so quickly, so they bred their crops from these. Soon they

▼ CATTLE ROCK PAINTING
When the people of the Sahara began to farm, their artists started to paint pictures of cattle. This example shows a herd of cattle, of the type that were kept more than 4,000 years ago. The painting also includes some of the people who herded them. It comes from a site in the Tassili mountains, in the central Sahara.

ON EARLY FARMS
Early farms looked quite unlike modern ones. The animals and plants were different, and the farmer and his family usually shared their house with the animals. There were no machines, just simple tools and a lot of hard work. The whole family helped, especially at busy times such as harvest. Even young children lent a hand, which was good training for when they would be farmers themselves.

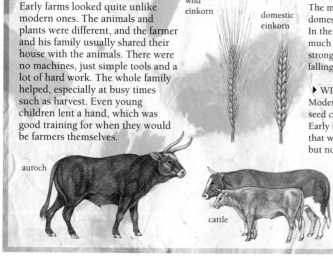

wild einkorn

domestic einkorn

auroch

cattle

◀ WILD AND DOMESTIC WHEAT
The main difference between wild and domestic einkorn wheat is the seeds. In the domestic variety these are much larger. The plant's stalk is also stronger, which stops the seeds from falling off before the harvest.

▶ WILD AND DOMESTIC CORN
Modern domestic corn has a larger seed cob than the ancient wild variety. Early farmers probably bred corn cobs that were larger than the wild varieties but not as big as today's giant cobs.

wild corn

domestic corn

◀ WILD AND DOMESTIC CATTLE
The wild auroch was the ancestor of early farm cattle. Bones found by archaeologists show that early domesticated cattle were smaller than the wild ones. But early farmers probably tried different sizes to see which suited them best.

◀ A FARMING VILLAGE
The first farming villages in Turkey were small clusters of mud-brick houses, where people and animals lived close together for safety. In the hot, dry summers, the village streets were baked hard and dusty, but in the winter they became a mass of puddles and sticky mud. These farmers kept goats and cattle descended from the wild aurochs.

had developed a new species, domesticated einkorn wheat, with seeds that broke away only during threshing.

Early farmers bred their animals in a similar way, selecting the beasts with the features they wanted and breeding from them. But the changes to the animal species were less dramatic than with the crops. The pigs farmed in the Fertile Crescent, for example, were much smaller and more like wild boars than modern domestic pigs. Cattle, too, were smaller than modern cows, and sheep and goats looked like the wild species.

Most early domestic animals were smaller than their wild cousins. This is probably because farmers bred good-tempered, docile creatures that were less aggressive and easier to handle than wild animals. Instead of choosing large specimens, farmers would have selected animals that produced the best-tasting meat or the highest yield of milk. Gradually, the farmers built up knowledge and experience, and they must have discovered that the smaller animals often had the features they wanted.

▲ PLANT DOMESTICATION
Farmers in different parts of the world grew different types of crops. In each area, one or two crops became the most commonly grown. They were varieties that were easy to grow in that particular area and provided a good basic crop.

Key Dates

- 9000 B.C. Sheep domesticated in northern Mesopotamia.

- 8000 B.C. First domesticated cereals grown around Jericho.

- 7000 B.C. Sheep and goats kept in the eastern Mediterranean.

- 7000 B.C. Barley grown in the Fertile Crescent. Emmer wheat in Palestine. Einkorn wheat in Turkey and Mesopotamia.

- 7000 B.C. Pigs are domesticated in southern Turkey.

- 6000 B.C. Cattle kept by farmers in north Africa and the eastern Mediterranean.

The Coming of Trade

▲ DAGGER
This dagger, with its long flint blade and its snake-shaped handle, was probably made for decorative effect rather than for use in battle.

FARMING MADE SOME PEOPLE well-fed, rich, and successful. They could trade the extra food they produced in exchange for luxury goods. Soon, this became a way of life for many farmers, and trading towns began to appear in the Fertile Cresecent and in Anatolia (Turkey). Most of these early towns disappeared long ago. As one set of mud-brick buildings fell into disrepair, they were knocked down. People built new houses on top of the old foundations. This happened many times over hundreds of years, and the town's ground level gradually rose as each group of houses was replaced. When a town was finally abandoned, the ruins, with their buildup of floor levels, was left in the form of a mound. In Syria and Palestine this type of ancient mound is called a tell. In Turkey it is known as a hüyük.

One of the most famous of these early town mounds is Çatal Hüyük in central Turkey. When archaeologists began to dig this mound, they found that it concealed an ancient town, occupied by a trading people who lived there between 7000 and

▶ BUILDING WORK
Clay was the main material for building in early trading towns of the Middle East. It could be molded into brick shapes while wet and left to dry in the sun. Surfaces were plastered to give a weatherproof finish outside and a smooth surface for decoration within.

6000 B.C. The countryside around the town was rich farming land. Charred remains from the town have shown that the people grew wheat, barley, lentils, and other vegetables, as well as eating such fruit as apples and wild nuts such as almonds.

The people of Çatal Hüyük probably traded in food products and raw materials for making tools. A favorite material was obsidian, a black glass formed naturally in volcanoes. Archaeologists have found a range of different tools and weapons made of flint and obsidian on the site.

The houses of Çatal Hüyük were built of mud brick. They were square or rectangular and built close together. One amazing feature of the town was that it had no streets. People entered their houses from the flat

MYSTERIES OF A TURKISH TOWN

There are still many mysteries surrounding the town of Çatal Hüyük in central Turkey, in spite of all the work of the archaeologists. No one knows for sure the meaning of the wall paintings in many of the rooms that have been excavated. The bulls, birds, leopards, and human figures were probably gods. However, it is not clear what the gods stood for, or how they were worshiped.

▲ BULL PAINTING
This mural is from a shrine at Çatal Hüyük. It shows a group of people baiting a gigantic bull. Bulls had religious significance because they were associated with a male god.

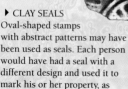

▶ CLAY SEALS
Oval-shaped stamps with abstract patterns may have been used as seals. Each person would have had a seal with a different design and used it to mark his or her property, as proof of ownership.

▶ BIRD WALL-PAINTING
These birds are probably vultures. People in some cultures left their dead out of doors until vultures had picked away the flesh.

roofs, stepping down wooden ladders to the floor below. Defending such places was easy.

Many houses contained at least one room set aside for religious ceremonies. These rooms, or shrines, are decorated with bulls' heads made of plaster and fitted with real bulls' horns. They also have wall paintings of animals and figures. Many of the figures are female, and archaeologists have also found more than 50 small

statues of pregnant women, suggesting that the people worshiped a mother goddess.

In addition, the shrines contain platforms that may have been used as altars in some form of religious ceremony. When residents of Çatal Hüyük died, their bodies were left in the open air, where the flesh was removed by the vultures. Then their relatives brought the bones back into the town and buried them beneath these platforms.

Ladder gives access to roof.

Flat roof provides work space and route to neighboring houses.

Decorated room used as religious shrine.

of made of ers of ber, reeds, d mud.

◀ TOWN HOUSES
Houses at Çatal Hüyük were made mainly from mud brick. This material was even used for fixtures such as benches and hearths. The houses were packed closely together with only a few courtyards between them. This made the town compact and helped to make it easier to defend, with few corners where enemies or wild beasts could lurk.

◀ EXCAVATING A SITE
The most common way for archaeologists to dig is to make a trench, a rectangular hole across the site. They can find remains from different periods because these lie in bands like a layer cake, revealing small areas across a broad time span. When there are many remains of buildings and other structures, such as at Çatal Hüyük, archaeologists will sometimes excavate to a shallow depth, over a broader area to cover more of the site.

Key Dates

- 8000B.C. Trade begins to develops in the Fertile Crescent and Anatolia.

- 7000B.C. Çatal Hüyük becomes important as a town and trading center.

- 7000B.C. Jericho expands; religious rituals include decorating skulls with plaster and shells.

- 6800B.C. Pottery is widely used in the eastern Mediterranean.

- 6500B.C. More elaborate burials at settlements such as Çatal Hüyük and Jericho show that some people were more important than others.

- 5000B.C. Trade links established between Turkey and the eastern Mediterranean.

Pots and Potters

▲ PAINTED POTTERY
The earliest pottery was plain, but potters soon learned how to paint their wares to make them more attractive. This pot is from an early farming community in Europe.

WE TAKE POTTERY, SUCH as cups, bowls, mugs, and plates, for granted. Before pottery was invented, our earliest ancestors used hollowed-out stone containers and woven baskets. The first pottery was probably made around 10,500 B.C. Pots are made from clay, which was dug from the ground, so they are cheap. They could be made in a variety of shapes and sizes, and held liquids as well as dry foods. Once people had discovered how to make pots, they never stopped finding new uses for them.

Pottery was probably discovered by accident. Early peoples baked bread and other foods in ovens which they made from earth. They piled up a mound of clay and made a hollow center in which they lit a fire. Inside, it became very hot. Eventually someone must have noticed that the sides of the clay oven had hardened with the heat.

It was probably some time before anyone had the idea of using this hardened clay to make containers. The earliest pots so far discovered come from Japan. From Japan, knowledge of pottery may have spread to China, where slightly more recent vessels have been found. However, in the rest of Asia, Europe, and Africa, pottery is much more recent. It is possible that it may have been discovered independently, as it was in America.

The first pots were made by the coiling process. The potter made a long, thin sausage of clay and looped it in a circle, spiraling upward to make the sides of the pot. Another ancient technique was to form pots by using a stone mold which was removed when the potter achieved the right shape. Much later, some time after 3000 B.C., the potter's wheel was invented. This device is still used by potters all over

◀ TERRACOTTA FIGURE
Pottery can be molded into all sorts of shapes, not only containers. People soon realized that they could use it to make small, portable statues. These were common among early farming communities, and archaeologists have excavated shrines with large numbers of these figures.

POTS AND POTTERS

In hunter-gatherer societies, people generally collected food as they needed it. Farming produced a glut of food at harvest time. People now needed containers to store this food, so pottery and farming flourished at the same time. The earliest pottery is unglazed. This means that it absorbs moisture, so that it is best used for dry goods such as grain and other solid foods.

◀ UNGLAZED POTS
Simple unglazed storage jars are still made in many parts of the world. These jars, elegantly shaped and decorated with patterns made by the potters' fingertips, come from Ghana. Pots like this are sometimes given a colorful glaze.

▲ ROUND-BASED POT
This is one of the oldest pots so far discovered by archaeologists. It comes from Nasunahara, Japan, and dates to around 10,500 B.C. The pot has a beaded pattern in bands around the rim.

▶ JOMON POT, JAPAN
Jomon or cord-marked pottery was produced in Japan around 10,000 B.C. The clay was coiled into shape, and the pots had pointed bases. They were probably hardened by heating on an open fire, rather than by firing in an enclosed kiln like later pots. This pot, used as a storage jar, stands about 9 inches high.

the world. The finished pots were fired and hardened in a kiln, which was similar to an ancient oven.

One advantage of pottery is that it is extremely long-lasting, and pots have survived to provide evidence for archaeologists. Each region and period has its own style of pottery. The color of the clay, the thickness of the pot, the style of decoration all vary from place to place and time to time. An archaeologist can often tell, even from a fragment of pottery, when and where it was made. They can therefore give a date to the sites where they find pots. Pots of foreign origin also provide clues as to trade and links between various countries.

▲ POTTERS AT WORK
The potter in the foreground is making a pot by coiling clay. She has prepared long, sausage-shaped pieces of clay and wound them around to build up the shape of the vessel. When she is happy with the overall shape, she will moisten her fingers and rub the surface of the pot to make it smooth. She may then make handles and stick them to the sides.

▲ EARLY POTTERY SITES
Archaeologists have discovered many remains of both early pottery and kilns in China and Japan. These areas continued to be at the forefront of developments in pottery until the 1800s. Kilns, glazing, and, much later, waterproof porcelain, were all discovered and first used in the Far East.

Key Dates

- 10,500 B.C. First Japanese pottery.
- 7000 B.C. Unbaked, sun-dried clay vessels made in Syria and Turkey.
- 7000 B.C. Hunter-fishers of southern Sahara are the first potters in Africa.
- 6500 B.C. First European pottery.
- 6000 B.C. Fishing communities in southern China make pottery.
- 3500 B.C. The tournette, a simple device for turning a pot, appears in Mesopotamia and Egypt.
- 3000 B.C. Potter's wheel invented in the Middle East.
- 1500 B.C. Glazed pottery which is resistant to water made in China.

European Settlements

▲ GREEK HOUSE
Early Greek farmers built small one-roomed houses with sloping thatched roofs. They often included a clay bin so that they could store their grain indoors. This house is from the village of Nea Nikomedeia in Greece.

FARMING SEEMS TO HAVE spread to Europe from the east, from around 7000B.C. It reached Europe from Turkey and then spread westward toward the Atlantic coast.

Then, as now, the European climate and landscape varied greatly. In the Balkans, where farming in Europe started, it was dry, and the land was suitable for sheep and goats, as well as for cereal growing. In northern Europe, early farmers led a very different life. The weather was colder, the soil heavier, and much of the ground was covered with forest. This was not good country for sheep and goats, so pig-rearing and cattle-herding were more popular. People could grow cereal crops, but the heavier soil was harder to cultivate than in the south. Gradually, over many centuries, the northerners developed strains of cereals that could grow in the heavy soil.

The woods of the north had many benefits. They were good foraging-grounds for pigs, and also provided a variety of food plants for people. They also sheltered animals, such as deer and wild boar, that could be hunted for both food and skins. The northern

Europeans continued to hunt and gather to add variety to the food they produced on their farms.

The plentiful timber was also useful for building. The farmers of central and northern Europe cut down trees to make a stout framework for the walls and roofs

▲ FARMING SETTLEMENT
A small farming village in western Britain consisted of a few round thatched houses clustered together. Next to the houses were fields for animals and crops. A trackway gave access to the fields and connected this village with its neighbors.

CRAFTS OF THE FARMERS

With the settled way of life that came with farming, people began to develop their craft skills. Among the most important were building and pottery. These early farmers were skilled woodworkers. They made fences, tools, and containers.

▲ RAISED PATHWAY
People sometimes built farming villages in marshy land. They made wooden walkways raised on posts so that they could cross the swamps safely.

face pot, Hungary

Bandkeramik pot, Germany

▲ DECORATED POTS
Potters decorated pots by drawing patterns or simplified faces in the damp clay. Another design was made up of lines and dots in a style known by the German name *Bandkeramik*, meaning "banded pottery."

▲ SEATED FIGURE
This pottery statuette from a farming site in Hungary shows a man holding a sickle. He may be a grain god, or just an ordinary farmer.

of their homes. They used split logs to make the walls and plastered them over with daub, a mixture of mud and straw, to fill the gaps. This helped to keep out drafts. The roofs, which had a steep pitch to throw off snow and rain, were thatched. Some of these houses were up to 150 feet in length and are known as longhouses. They were Europe's first sizable, permanent dwellings. Besides a large room for the family, they usually also contained a storeroom

for crops and an area for cattle. Sometimes humans and animals shared the same room. It was cramped and smelly, but people put up with this to make sure their animals were safe.

Farming villages became established in many river valleys. People used the rivers to travel between neighboring villages to trade. As they traveled, they also exchanged ideas about new discoveries and inventions. As a result, pottery techniques and styles improved and spread, and new ideas about crop and animal cultivation were shared. The people of Europe were developing skills that would stay in use for thousands of years.

◀ EUROPEAN FARMERS
At Langweiler, Germany, farmers build a longhouse for their family and animals. They have constructed the walls and are now thatching the roof. To do this they have gathered reeds from a nearby river. Reeds make a longer-lasting thatch than grass or straw.

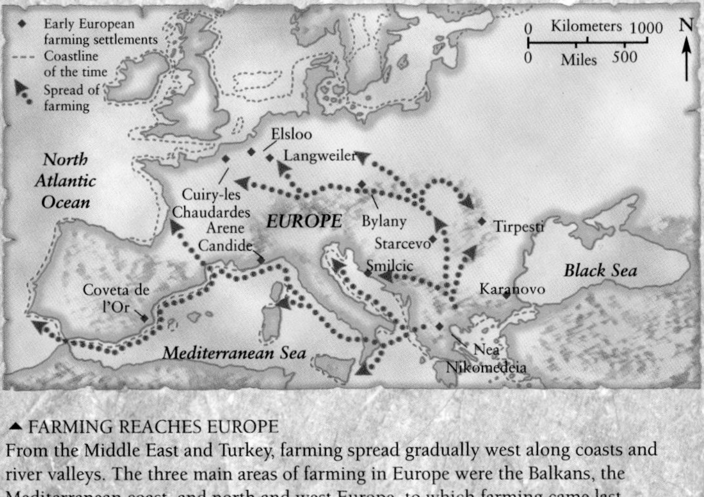

▲ FARMING REACHES EUROPE
From the Middle East and Turkey, farming spread gradually west along coasts and river valleys. The three main areas of farming in Europe were the Balkans, the Mediterranean coast, and north and west Europe, to which farming came last.

Map labels: Early European farming settlements; Coastline of the time; Spread of farming; North Atlantic Ocean; Elsloo; Langweiler; Cuiry-les-Chaudardes; Arene Candide; EUROPE; Bylany; Starcevo; Smilcic; Tirpesti; Coveta de l'Or; Karanovo; Black Sea; Mediterranean Sea; Nea Nikomedeia; Kilometers 1000; Miles 500; N

Key Dates

- 7000B.C. Farming reaches eastern Europe, probably from Turkey.
- 6200B.C. Farming begins in Sicily and southern Italy.
- 5400B.C. Farming spreads across northern Europe, from Hungary, through Germany, to the Netherlands.
- 5000B.C. Farming communities such as Langweiler are thriving.
- 5000B.C. Farming has spread across southern Europe and has reached the south of France.
- 4000B.C. Farming established in most of Europe.

Asian Communities

Good soil and useful local crops encouraged Asian people to begin farming. This is how agriculture began in eastern Asia, in places such as the highlands of northwest and central India and areas around the banks of the Yellow River in China. Both regions had good natural resources and a climate suitable for farming. Archaeologists have found the remains of several early farming villages in both places.

▲ HARPOON HEADS, CHINA
Items like these bone harpoon points from the farming site at Banpo, China, show that hunting and river fishing were still key sources of food.

Central India had grassy uplands suitable for cattle grazing and river banks with rich soil for crops. Farming began early here, around 7000B.C. Barley was a popular crop, and farmers herded cattle, goats, and sheep on the hills. In some places, people gathered together to build villages. One of the first was called Mehrgarh, a cluster of houses by the river Bolan in northwest India. The houses were square or rectangular, and built of mud bricks plastered with mud. The flat roofs were made of reed thatch supported on long wooden poles. Inside, there were several rooms. Thick walls and small windows kept

▲ RICE FARMER
When the people had worked out how to cultivate the waterlogged fields of southern China and south-east Asia, rice became the staple crop of these areas.

the houses warm in winter and cool in summer. The style remained much the same for the next 1,000 years.

Communities like Mehrgarh grew. People built storehouses for grain to ensure a reserve when supplies became short. Some members of the community grew rich, perhaps by trading. Their graves contain favorite possessions, such as beads of shell or limestone.

Meanwhile, agriculture was developing in China. Here, millet was the favored crop, and the pig was the

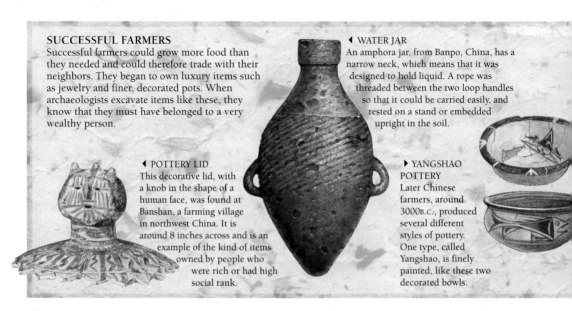

SUCCESSFUL FARMERS
Successful farmers could grow more food than they needed and could therefore trade with their neighbors. They began to own luxury items such as jewelry and finer, decorated pots. When archaeologists excavate items like these, they know that they must have belonged to a very wealthy person.

◀ WATER JAR
An amphora jar, from Banpo, China, has a narrow neck, which means that it was designed to hold liquid. A rope was threaded between the two loop handles so that it could be carried easily, and rested on a stand or embedded upright in the soil.

◀ POTTERY LID
This decorative lid, with a knob in the shape of a human face, was found at Banshan, a farming village in northwest China. It is around 8 inches across and is an example of the kind of items owned by people who were rich or had high social rank.

▶ YANGSHAO POTTERY
Later Chinese farmers, around 3000B.C., produced several different styles of pottery. One type, called Yangshao, is finely painted, like these two decorated bowls.

first creature to be domesticated. Farmers also grew vegetables, such as cabbages, and harvested fruit, such as plums. Later, they began to grow rice, which became the staple in most of eastern Asia. Rice was especially successful in southern China, where the ground was wetter.

Chinese farmers quickly learned that their soils needed a rest after a season of cultivation. They developed a method of farming that switched from one field to another. This allowed the land to have a fallow period, in which the land was not plowed or sown. They found that by leaving a long fallow period between periods of growing, the land could be restored. Much later, around 1100B.C., they began to alternate crops of millet and soy beans. The bean plants brought goodness back to the soil, so that it was less important to have a fallow period.

Techniques of farming spread steadily across China. Wet farming techniques needed for rice were passed from south to north, along with strains of rice that grew more successfully in the north. China also had contact with Korea and Japan. These two areas had successful hunting and fishing communities. Agriculture did not become established there until much later.

straw thatch · plastered wall · supporting pole · central hearth

▲ FARMER'S HUT, BANPO
Chinese archaeologists found the remains of a cluster of houses belonging to the early farming community of Banpo in northern China, dating from about 6000B.C. The buildings were oblong or round. They were built with a stout wooden framework filled in with a basketweave of thin branches. This was plastered over to make a smooth, weather-resistant wall. Thatch covered the roofs, but there was a central hole to let smoke escape from the fire in the floor below.

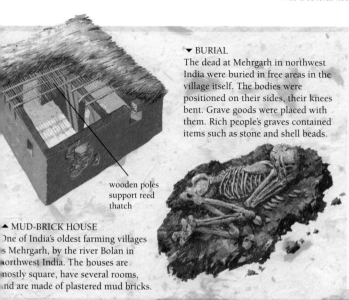

▼ BURIAL
The dead at Mehrgarh in northwest India were buried in free areas in the village itself. The bodies were positioned on their sides, their knees bent. Grave goods were placed with them. Rich people's graves contained items such as stone and shell beads.

wooden poles support reed thatch

▲ MUD-BRICK HOUSE
One of India's oldest farming villages is Mehrgarh, by the river Bolan in northwest India. The houses are mostly square, have several rooms, and are made of plastered mud bricks.

Key Dates

- 7000B.C. Barley growing begins in India.
- 6000B.C. Indian farmers build storehouses for their surplus food.
- 6000B.C. Millet is the main crop of farmers in northern China.
- 5500B.C. Date palms are cultivated in Mesopotamia.
- 5500B.C. Indian farmers produce their own strains of wheat.
- 5000B.C. Farmers of the Yangtze Delta area cultivate rice.
- 3500B.C. Trade networks link the regions of China.
- 3000B.C. Millet grown in Korea.

The Americas

People of southwestern North America made figures like this split-twig deer. These figures date to a period after 3500B.C. and are often found near hunters' weapons and equipment.

WHETHER THEY WERE fishing or harpooning seals in the far north, hunting buffalo on the Great Plains, or gathering food in the south, the people of the Americas followed the food supply. Because crops grew in the least extreme weather conditions, they also had to move with the seasons. They became used to a restless life.

In Central America, environmental changes were often fast and unpredictable. Torrential rain was followed by baking sun. The people here longed for more control over their food supply, and they turned to agriculture before the rest of the Americas. However, they still needed good weather for their crops, which is perhaps why so many of them worshiped gods of rain and sun. The farmers hoped that worshiping these deities would bring them the most favorable conditions throughout the agricultural year.

One of the earliest crops in Central America was corn (maize), a plant that has been important in American farming ever since. It was developed from a

▲ HUT AND HUNTER
In eastern North America, hunters often built short-term shelters, like this hut. They made a framework of thin wooden poles, joined together at the top. This they covered with grass. Huts like this could catch fire easily, so the hearth was outside.

local wild grass called teosinte. Farmers tried different varieties, choosing the plants that grew best in local conditions. This proved a successful approach, and maize farming spread quite quickly.

Farther north, in what is now the southwestern United States, the first farmers experimented with various types of gourd and with plants such as sunflower and sumpweed. As the farmers of Central America began to trade more widely, they took their

AMERICAN FARMERS

The Americas contain a variety of different climates and environments, all with their own native plant species. For the early farmers, the challenge was to choose the best plants for their own region. Often this was simply a question of selecting from local species that were known to do well. But sometimes an imported crop, such as cotton in southern North America, was a success.

◀ POTATOES
Between 3000–2500B.C., farmers in the hills of the Andes were growing the potato. For thousands of years, this useful root crop was grown only in South America, and many varieties of potato are still found only in the Andes.

▲ STONE WEIGHTS
Hunters in Kentucky attached these stone weights to the handles of their spear-throwers. This made their spears travel much farther and faster. As a result, when a spear hit an animal it was much more powerful.

◀ CLAY FIGURINE
Mysterious statuettes like this one have been found in numerous North American settlements. They have little in the way of modeling or facial features, so it is impossible to tell whether they represent male or female figures. They are made of clay and decorated with lines and dots. The clay was not fired, though; it simply became hard with age. No one knows what these figures were for.

domesticated maize, beans, and squash with them, and these joined the local plants to become staple crops in the north. For many people in the southwest, the plants were a welcome addition to foraged foods.

In South America people tried to cultivate a variety of crops, including gourds, squashes, manioc, potatoes, and various types of bean. In each area, they selected the best plants for local conditions and tried different growing methods over thousands of years. The region where farming caught on most quickly was Peru. In the Andes Mountains, hunter-gatherers began to grow crops such as gourds and beans to add to their existing diet. They carried on using this mixed form of food supply for many thousands of years.

In the coastal areas, rivers had created narrow valleys as they flowed off the mountains to the sea. In the rich soil found in these valleys, people began to grow squashes and peppers, to which they later added maize. They also developed methods of irrigation to bring water from the rivers to their fields.

Animal farming was at first less popular in the Americas than in other parts of the world. There were few native species that were easy to farm. But in the Andes Mountains one species, the llama, was valued for its wool and milk, as well as being used as a beast of burden. The people of the Americas developed a variety of crops and farming techniques, but in many places wild foods were still widely available, and many groups carried on their lifestyle of hunting and gathering.

▼ RIVER TRANSPORTATION
Simple wooden canoes provided transportation along North America's rivers. There were various ways of making these. They could be "dug-outs," made by hollowing out a log. Another design was made of thin tree bark attached to a wooden frame.

▼ SUNFLOWERS
This giant member of the daisy family is found mainly in North America. Farmers prized it for its seeds, which can be eaten. Later they learned how to extract the oil from the seeds, using it for cooking. Some species also have edible roots.

▶ COTTON
This valuable crop was first cultivated in two separate areas, Peru and Ecuador in South America and Mexico in North America. From Mexico, traders took it farther north, where farmers in the Southwest later began to grow the plant.

Key Dates

- 8500 B.C. Agriculture established in Peru. Crops grown include squash, beans, and grasses.

- 7000 B.C. In Central America people gather avocado, chillies, squash, and beans. These are plants farmers will begin to cultivate in the next 2,000 years.

- 6300 B.C. Farmers in Peru grow various root crops, such as oca and ulluco.

- 5400 B.C. The use of llamas for wool, milk and transportation is found in the Andes.

- 5000 B.C. Mexican farmers grow maize.

- 5000 B.C. Domesticated plants of Central America, such as the bottle gourd, begin to spread to North America.

Hunting and Gathering

▲ GIRAFFE
Artists painted both farm animals and the hunters' favorite quarry on the walls of rock shelters in the Sahara Desert. The giraffe was one of the creatures that people living in Africa both herded and hunted during prehistoric times.

FARMING WAS NOT FOR everyone. Hunting and gathering can provide a steady, reliable source of food as long as there are not too many people living in a small area. Africa is one part of the world where some peoples made the change to farming while others continued to hunt and gather for much longer.

After the final Ice Age, the Sahara was a much damper, greener environment than it is today. It became the scene for some of Africa's earliest experiments in farming. Rock paintings show how the people began to herd cattle, together with other local species such as giraffe.

When the Sahara dried out and gradually turned to desert, most agricultural activity was pushed to the south, between the Sahara and the Equator. This was where the climate allowed farmers to develop crops such as yam and

sorghum, a cereal crop that was suited to warm places. This area became the heartland of African farming.

Still farther south, people carried on hunting and gathering. They ate a number of local plants, especially various palms and a shrub called bauhinia. In addition, they found out how to use other plants for more specialized purposes. A good example was the bottle gourd, which was suitable for making into containers.

The African hunter-gatherers also improved their tools. To make knives, they used tiny blades of sharp flint, which they glued into wooden handles using natural tree resin. They also carved hooks from bone for fishing. Such uses of the materials around them show how highly adapted they were to their environment.

Australia was another place where the traditional lifestyle of hunting and gathering continued. To begin with,

◀ ZULU HUNTER
Today, some African peoples still get some of their food by hunting, but now their spears are tipped with metal rather than the stone of earlier times.

USEFUL SPECIES
The early hunter-gatherers of Africa and Australia had a vast knowledge of plants. When they came across a new species they would try it out. This was a dangerous process, as many plants were poisonous. They gradually discovered plants that were good to eat and others that worked as medicines. Modern scientists are still investigating the plant medicines used by the world's hunter-gatherer peoples.

◀ ALMONDS
Nuts, such as almonds, that are native to North Africa and the Middle East, are a nutritious food. Gatherers made a point of going to the forest when they were in season. Nuts are easy to store and contain plenty of energy-building protein, useful to hunter-gatherers when meat is in short supply.

▶ JUNIPER BERRIES
Gatherers soon knew everything about the plants in their area. They discovered that some plants, though not good to eat, had other useful properties. Berries such as juniper, which grows all over the northern hemisphere, were valued for their perfume and their use in medicine.

◀ GOURD
Some species of gourd were very useful. When the flesh had been eaten, the outer shells made excellent containers. People made bowls with the larger fruit, while using smaller ones to make items such as dippers and cups.

people stayed near the coast, living on fish, eels, and, especially, shellfish. Remains of the shells, left in dumps that archaeologists call middens, have been found along both the north and southeast coasts. As time went on, the native Australians explored the river valleys, moving gradually inland. People discovered that cereal plants such as millet made good food. They developed hunting skills that enabled them to survive when they moved even farther inland toward Australia's hot and dry interior.

The early Australians traveled for miles, exchanging tools and shell jewelry, and creating the beautiful rock art, which can still be found all over the country. As they did this, they were also developing a complex series of myths about their ancestry that reflected their hunting and gathering lifestyle. Most important of all are the stories of Dreamtime, the period when the earth and the spirits of people were created. These myths held, and still hold, great religious significance for native Australians, and they reveal a people of profound beliefs.

▲ HUNTER-GATHERERS
This group of hunter-gatherers have found an area rich in food and have made a camp with a brushwood shelter that they will occupy for weeks or even months. While two men butcher the antelope they have killed, another group of people returns from gathering vegetables and wood for the fire on which they will cook the meat.

▶ ENGRAVED PEARL SHELL
In societies that did not use metals, all sorts of items were adapted for use as jewelry. This ornament, engraved with abstract designs, was made by native Australians from a piece of pearl shell.

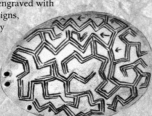

◀ BARK PAINTING
A hunter throws his spear at a crane in this bark painting from Australia's Northern Territory. This style of painting is known as "x-ray," because the designs on the crane depict the bird's insides.

Key Dates

- 10,000 B.C. Obsidian, a type of volcanic glass, used to make tools in the Rift Valley area of eastern Africa.

- 9000 B.C. People move into the Sahara region; increased rainfall allows grasslands to grow along the edges of what is now desert.

- 7000 B.C. African communities in the Sahara begin making pottery.

- 6000 B.C. People start herding cattle in some parts of the Sahara region.

- 4000 B.C. Sahara reaches its wettest, most temperate conditions, with Lake Chad at its largest.

- 3500 B.C. Ostrich eggshell beads become popular as necklaces in eastern Africa.

The First Metalworkers

▲ GOLD BULL
The settlement of Varna, on the Black Sea, was one of Europe's first metal-working sites. Hundreds of gold ornaments, bracelets and beads have been discovered there.

As they created art on surfaces in caves, ancient peoples must have seen gold. They would also have seen copper, as it has a greenish tinge in the rock. Deposits of metal in rock are rare and difficult to extract. It was a long time before anyone worked out how to remove the material and then to work it into something useful. Eventually, someone found a place where there was enough metal to remove and found that it could be hammered into shape. Metal was beaten into ornamental objects such as beads, which were soon highly valued.

When craftworkers started to make pottery, they built kilns that could reach temperatures as high as 1,470°F. Before long, they found that heating certain rocks, or ores, in the kiln melted the metal they contained, so that it could be poured off and collected. They had discovered the process called smelting. This made it possible to extract much larger amounts of metal from the ore. People could make all kinds of items, such as jewelry and tools, out of copper instead

▲ BRONZE AGE SETTLEMENT
Most of the people of Bronze Age Europe lived in small villages with thatched houses, like those built by the first farmers. An area would be set aside for metalworking away from the houses, so that there was less risk of fire.

THE MAGIC OF METAL
The first metals must have seemed like magic. By heating the ore, the metalworker could make metal appear, apparently out of nowhere. It would first be seen in hot, liquid form, then it would miraculously set when it cooled. Copper and gold glittered beautifully in the light, so people found these metals very attractive.

▼ LONG-HORNED OXEN
Small, precious objects, such as pieces of jewelry, were among the first items to be made of metal, because they did not use too much of it. Early metalworkers could produce work of great skill, as these copper oxen found in Poland show.

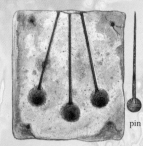

mold

pin

◀ MOLD AND PIN
A Bronze Age mold and matching pin show how the process of casting could be used to produce a number of items at speed—in this case three pins at the same time. The small holes at each corner would have matched with bumps in the other half of the mold, to ensure a perfect fit.

▶ COPPER AND TIN
The first important alloy was bronze, a mix of copper and tin. Tin is not common, so bronze developed slowly where there were good tin deposits—China, the Middle East, and parts of France, Germany, and Britain.

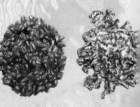

copper

tin

▶ CASTING

Metal items, such as tools and weapons, could be made by casting. The metalworker prepared a stone mold in two parts that fitted together exactly. When the halves were joined and secured with twine, the hollow inside the mold had the shape of the object to be cast. Hot molten metal was poured into the mold through a hole in the top. When the metal had cooled and set, the metalworker took the mold apart to reveal the object. The same mold could be used again and again.

of other materials. There was still a problem, however. Metals such as gold and copper were easy to work, but they were soft. They made good jewelry, but poor tools. The solution was to combine one metal with another to make an alloy that was hard-wearing. The best alloy discovered in the ancient world was bronze. This was made by mixing copper with a little tin. It was tough, quite easy to work, had a pleasant, gold-colored appearance, and could be sharpened.

Bronze became a popular material for jewelry, tools, and weapons. Sometimes, once a metalworker had smelted some copper and mixed in some tin, he would let the molten metal set into a bar and then hammer it into shape. Liquid metal can also be cast in a mold to produce all sorts of complex shapes. Casting was popular because it was easy to produce many identical items using the same mould. However, since hammering hardened the metal, this method was still used to make objects such as weapons, which had to be very strong.

Metal technology probably began in the Middle East around 3000B.C., and spread to other parts of the world during the next 2,000 years. The development of bronzeworking is so important that historians sometimes call this period the Bronze Age. Bronze did not reach all parts of the world. There was no Bronze Age in Australia, South America, or many parts of Africa. In such places, although people may have used gold or copper occasionally, they mostly made do with the stone technology they had developed. They had to wait until the coming of iron before they could take full advantage of metals.

▲ THE SPREAD OF COPPER IN EUROPE
In Europe, copper working began in two main centers, Iberia (southern Spain) and the Balkans, where plenty of the metal was available. From these centers, archaeologists have mapped and dated discoveries of bronze objects. This gives a rough idea of how knowledge of the craft spread across the European continent.

Key Dates

- 9000B.C. Copper used in some parts of Asia for tools and weapons.

- 6000B.C. Smelting and casting are developed in the Middle East and southeastern Europe.

- 4000B.C. Knowledge of metalworking begins spreading to Europe, Asia, and North Africa.

- 3000B.C. Bronze technology develops in the Middle East.

- 3000–1000B.C. Better trade routes enable bronzeworking techniques to spread across much of Europe.

- 2000B.C. Bronzeworking develops in China.

- 2000B.C. Bronze is used widely in Asia for everyday tools and weapons.

Megaliths

▲ NIGHT SKY
People have always looked to the sky in their religion. Most stone circles and rows of standing stones are arranged to line up with the Sun, Moon, or stars.

Towering standing stones, massive stone circles, and vast rows of stones are the most awesome of all prehistoric remains. Some of them are so huge that no one knows how Bronze Age people ever managed to build them. Because they are so big, they are known as megaliths, a term that comes from two Greek words meaning huge stones.

Another mystery is exactly what these vast monuments were for. Archaeologists think they may have been used for religious ceremonies. The stones are often lined up with yearly movements of the Sun and stars, so the ceremonies were almost certainly linked to the calendar and the seasons. They may have been fertility ceremonies, relating the crop-growing season to the annual movements of the stars.

There are two famous groups of megaliths in Europe, one on England's Salisbury Plain, the other in Brittany, France. Many of the British monuments are stone circles the most famous are at Stonehenge and Avebury. The main monument in Brittany is a series of rows, or alignments, of stones near the village of Carnac. In both cases there are many other prehistoric monuments nearby, such as smaller circles and alignments, earthworks, burial mounds, and single standing stones. Together these structures make up

▲ BUILDING STONEHENGE
Stonehenge in Wiltshire, England, the greatest of all the stone circles, was built with the simplest technology. The builders probably used sleds or rollers to move the stones, each weighing about 40 tons, about 15 miles to the site, before heaving them into place with a combination of ropes and levers.

THE CHANGING MONUMENTS
The megalithic monuments of Europe have stood for thousands of years, but they have not always looked the same. Archaeologists have found many holes in the ground where additional stones and wooden posts once stood, making these sites even more complex than they are today. The monuments were also altered throughout prehistory, with the removal of some stones and the addition of others.

◀ DOLMEN
Groups of stones like this are called dolmens. They started out covered with earth as the chambers of prehistoric burial mounds. When the mound was moved or eroded away, the roof and its supports were left.

▲ CALLANISH STONE CIRCLE
This is quite a small circle of 13 tall, thin stones. It is in the Hebrides islands, off Scotland, and is at the focal point of lines of standing stones. The stones, some of which are 15 feet high, were quarried only a short distance away from the site. Archaeologists have calculated that each of the stones could have been dragged along by about 20 people.

▶ FESTIVAL AT AVEBURY
Another British stone circle, at Avebury in Wiltshire, may been the scene of an annual harvest or farming festival like the one shown here. The form of the ritual is unknown, but there were probably processions, offerings, and observations of the stars or Moon.

entire regions that would have been known as holy places, landscapes devoted to religion.

The builders of the megalithic monuments had to move and lift huge stones, dig long ditches, and pile up enormous mounds of earth. Yet the people of the Bronze Age had no complex machinery, only rollers, levers, ropes, and simple hand tools. It must have taken the labor of hundreds of people over many years to move the stones. Clearly, a great deal of organization was needed, and probably a ruler with enough power to keep everyone at work on the task. Planning was also important, so that the builders could work out the precise positions for the stones. These vast temples suggest that Bronze Age societies were far more advanced than you would expect, considering the simple tools they had.

◀ MEGALITHIC SITES
Britain, Ireland and northern France are the main areas where megalithic monuments can be found. This probably shows that the people of these three areas were in regular contact, traveling across the English Channel and Irish Sea, when the megaliths were erected. They must have had similar religious beliefs and ceremonies, although we now know very little about these. There were once many more megaliths, but in the 1700s and 1800s farmers cleared away large numbers of these monuments from their fields.

Key Dates

- 4000B.C. Ditched enclosures common in many parts of Europe.

- 4000B.C. Long barrows and megalithic tombs become common for high-status burials in Europe.

- 3200B.C. People in Europe begin to build stone circles.

- 3000B.C. In Europe, much land is cleared for agriculture.

- 2100B.C. Stones added to a site originally made up of ditches and earth banks, make Stonehenge Britain's biggest megalithic site.

- 1500B.C. The age of stone circles and standing stones comes to an end.

Lake Villages

▲ POTTERY
The lake village people used lots of pottery vessels. Some were narrow-necked, like this jug, which was made for carrying water.

THE SHORES OF ALPINE LAKES in Europe are made up of bogs and marshland. They are difficult to cross and very hard to build on. Yet archaeologists have discovered the remains of several hundred Bronze Age villages in the European Alps. The small settlements, with their simple wooden houses, were in the middle of swamps by the shores of lakes such as Constance and Neuchâtel, on the borders of modern Switzerland, France, and Germany. Why did people put up with damp, boggy conditions?

The lakes themselves were rich in fish, which could be dried or smoked, to preserve them for times when food was less plentiful. Some way beyond the lake shores was grassland, which provided grazing for animals. The foothills of the Alps were thickly forested, offering a

good supply of wood for building and fuel. Most important of all, the swampy conditions made it very easy to defend the villages against enemies.

Many villages sprang up by the lakes. People cut down trees from the alpine foothills to build their houses. Roofs were thatched with reeds from the lakesides. Each house was raised above the marsh with stout wooden poles rammed deep into the earth. Wood was also used to make pathways across the swamp and to build strong fences around each village. Most villages

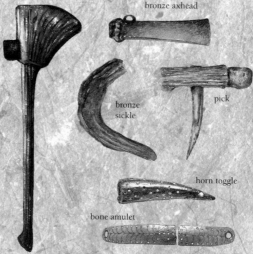

TOOLS FOR THE JOB

In prehistoric times, most of the lakeside region of Europe was wooded right down to the lake shores. So, before they could start building homes, the villagers had to clear away some of the trees and prepare logs for building. For this, they needed heavy stone axes with long wooden handles. Once they were settled, they could use lighter metal tools for everyday work in the fields and around the village.

▶ AX HANDLE
Waterlogged soil near the Swiss lakes has preserved ancient wooden objects, such as this ax handle. This gives us knowledge of craft skills that we lack for most prehistoric peoples.

bronze axhead

bronze sickle

pick

horn toggle

bone amulet

◀ TOOL KIT
After about 2000 B.C., the alpine lake people started to use bronze to make many of their tools. Axes for chopping and sickles for harvesting were two typical metal items. There were also picks with bone or antler handles.

◀ BONE AND HORN
Many items were made of these materials. Animal horn was a good material to make toggles to fasten coats and tunics. Bone could be carved into all sorts of shapes, including fastenings and pierced objects which may have been sacred charms.

were quite small, with up to 20 houses. Eventually, after 30 or 40 years, the wet ground made the poles supporting the houses rot. Either they were replaced or the people moved on to another site.

Trapped deep beneath the water, however, an amazing amount of evidence of these villages has been preserved. Archaeologists have brought to the surface some of the timbers from the houses and pathways, as well as bronze implements. In some cases even remains of the people's food and clothing have survived, preserved in the cold water.

Some of the settlements had at least one large house. This was probably the home of the village chief. Archaeologists have found decorated bronze weapons and jewelry in these houses, showing that these chiefs were rich and powerful.

▼ ON THE LAKESHORE
This view of a prehistoric lake village shows how close the inhabitants were to the resources they needed to live—reeds and fish in the lake itself, timber from the forests, and fertile fields nearby. For communities like this, easy access to these resources made it worthwhile to build in such a difficult, marshy area.

▲ REEDS
For thatched roofs, by far the best material is reed. It is strong and long-lasting and grows in abundance along the edges of lakes.

▼ LAKESIDE VILLAGE
Sites near lakes have always proved popular in places such as Austria, Switzerland, and their neighboring countries. Places such as Zurich, Neuchâtel, Lausanne, and Konstanz are all built by large lakes. Many of these modern towns and cities are built on the sites of prehistoric lake villages. The picture shows a lakeside village in the Austrian Alps. Today, many people like to visit lakeside sites because of the stunning scenery.

Key Dates

- 3000B.C. Trading villages well established on the shores of the Black Sea; the inhabitants work copper and gold and trade along the local rivers.

- 3000B.C. People settle along the shores of lakes in Europe's alpine region.

- 2000B.C. Substantial wooden villages are built by the settlers in alpine areas. The people purposely select sites that are easy to defend and learn how to fortify their villages with boundary fences.

- 1600B.C. The heyday of the lake villages comes to an end.

The Iron Age

▲ IRON DAGGER
Forged from iron and carried in a bronze sheath, this British dagger probably belonged to an important person such as a chief. It dates from the time when European society was led by warriors.

BRONZE WAS A USEFUL METAL, but it was not as hard as stone. Neither was it always easy to find the copper and tin needed to make it. Many people carried on using flint tools and weapons. Then, in around 1300 B.C., some metalworkers in the Middle East discovered iron.

Iron is a common metal in many parts of the world. It is easy to smelt, provided that the temperature in the furnace is high enough. It can be sharpened easily and can be strengthened by hammering. When metalworkers first began to smelt iron, they did not realize it was a common material. Because it was new and unusual, it was used for weapons carried by high-ranking men such as chiefs. Soon, however, they saw how common and useful iron was and began to make iron tools and weapons in large numbers.

Ironworking gradually spread throughout the Middle East and into southern Europe. Iron weapons helped empire-building peoples, such as the Hittites of Turkey, to conquer new territory. They helped the Greeks, who were building colonies around the Mediterranean, in much the same way. In India, where the people had found little copper, iron

▼ IRON AGE SETTLEMENT
When the people of Iron Age Europe built a fort, they defended it by building deep ditches. The earth from the ditches was thrown up to make massive banks, giving extra protection. Forts like this covered a huge area, with enough space for people, houses, and animals.

REMAINS FROM THE IRON AGE

Many of the most impressive remains from the Iron Age are actually made of bronze. Iron tools and weapons were made in large numbers, but most have rusted away. Bronze objects, on the other hand, are longer lasting, even if buried in the ground. As a result, many bronze items, buried in the graves of high-ranking chieftains, have survived.

◀ ▼ BROOCHES
Iron Age people fastened their clothes with brooches, which were usually made of bronze and could be very ornate. The fibula style had a long pin that worked like a modern safety pin.

fibula brooch   spectacle brooch

▶ LA TÈNE HORN
The curving, swirling lines of the decoration on the end of this horn are typical of the Celtic La Tène style, which developed during the late Iron Age in Europe. It is one of four horns made of bronze found in an Irish lake.

▲ BRONZE SHIELD
A shield, found in Battersea, London, was decorated by hammering the metal to make raised patterns. Colored glass and stones were added.

detail of trumpet end

made metal technology widely available for the very first time.

In Europe, iron transformed people's lives. It enabled the Celtic people, who lived in western Europe, to become warlike and powerful. They built large hill forts, protected by earthworks and fences, and fought off attackers with iron weapons. A whole village could fit into one hill fort, and these forts became bases for warrior chiefs.

The first phase of the European Iron Age is known as the Halstatt period, after a site in Austria where a number of iron swords were found. Halstatt chiefs grew rich, both from trading and from forcing neighbors to pay them tribute. Some chiefs even owned goods imported from as far away as Greece and Italy.

After about the 5th century B.C., the Celts began to produce metalwork beautifully decorated in a free, swirling style. This style is called La Tène, after the Swiss lakeside site where archaeologists have found many iron and bronze items.

By the time the Romans were building up their empire in Europe, the Celts were powerful enough to fight the Romans' armies and halt them for a while. The Celtic chiefs issued their own coinage, built strong forts, and traded with Rome in times of peace. For several centuries, these men of iron were Europe's strongest and most feared leaders.

▲ IRONWORKERS
In order to produce workable iron, the ore (the rock containing the metal) had to be heated to a high temperature. Early ironworkers made kilns of earth to contain the fire so that it could build up enough heat.

▲ IRON AGE SITES
Although Europe has perhaps the most famous of all Iron Age cultures, people in many other parts of the world discovered how to work iron. Eastern Asia and Africa were two areas that had notable Iron Age societies.

Key Dates

- 2000B.C. Middle Eastern people discover iron and make iron tools and weapons.

- 1000B.C. Ironworking established in central Europe.

- 800B.C. Beginning of Halstatt period.

- 600B.C. Iron discovered in China; hotter furnaces enable the Chinese to cast iron, something impossible in the west until much later.

- 500B.C. Ironworking begins in Africa.

- 500B.C. Ironworking well established in most of Europe.

- 450–100B.C. Fine metalwork of the La Tène period made in Europe.

The Birth of Civilization

▲ PAINTED POT
Pottery from the Mesopotamian cities is often of a very high quality: thin, well shaped, and with elegant decoration.

WHILE MANY OF THE EVENTS described in this book were happening, another development, more earth-shattering than all the rest, was beginning at different points on the globe. Small towns were growing into cities. Their inhabitants were putting up large temples and palaces, inventing written languages, and creating complex societies in which there were many different jobs for people to do. There were farmers, craftworkers, priests, governors, and kings. This new city-based way of life is what we now call civilization.

The place where civilization first began was Mesopotamia, the land between the Tigris and Euphrates rivers in what is now Iraq. This was part of the Fertile Crescent, where farming had started. It was the reliable food supply produced by farming that made the developments that followed possible.

As the farmers became more experienced, they worked out how to irrigate their fields so that they could bring water to the drier areas. This made the food supply more constant. The farmers could also increase

◀ WOMAN AND BABY
This figure of a mother holding a baby is made of clay. It dates from the 'Ubaid period, which lasted from 5500 to 4000B.C. At this time, towns were growing into cities, craftworkers were becoming more and more skilled, and local leaders were gaining in power.

the size of their fields by cultivating previously difficult areas.

At the same time, the people of Mesopotamia began to build large, comfortable mud brick houses. They created beautiful painted pottery, fine clay sculptures, intricate copper implements, and elegant jewelry with turquoise beads. People from other areas wanted these items, so the Mesopotamians traded with their neighbors, carrying their cargo by boat down the rivers and along the Persian Gulf. Gradually, the traders of Mesopotamia became rich, and their towns grew into cities. With cities came more power and more complex government. The priests, who were among the most powerful people, built bigger temples, another mark of civilization. Then came writing. At first, this was only a few simple symbols to show who

ARTS OF CIVILIZATION
One of the features of civilization was that society became more complex. In other words, it was divided into more social classes, with more powerful leaders and more difference between rich and poor. The rich people demanded better, more luxurious goods, from pots to jewelry, and in Mesopotamia this led to the growth of arts and crafts. Pottery, metalworking, building, and sculpture are all crafts that developed quickly at this time.

◀ POTTERY FRAGMENTS
Ancient rubbish heaps are treasure troves for archaeologists. Many pieces of broken pottery have been unearthed from the 'Ubaid period, from 5500B.C. to 4000B.C. They often have striking painted decoration.

◀ NECKLACES
Mesopotamian necklaces could have thousands of beads in several separate strings. The large one, found at a farming site called Choga Mami, has around 2,200 beads, crudely shaped from clay.

◀ WRITING
The scribes of Mesopotamia wrote by making marks in clay tablets with a wedge-shaped reed. This writing is called cuneiform, from a Greek word meaning wedge.

▶ HEAD FROM STATUETTE
Terracotta heads like these show the style of sculpture in Mesopotamia, with some features, such as the eyes, enlarged.

owned what. Later people developed more complicated writing systems that enabled people to record stories and religious texts.

The development of writing marks the end of prehistoric society. This happened at different times in different parts of the world. During the lifetimes of some of the prehistoric peoples, civilization was already present in Mesopotamia and other parts of the globe. Civilization came early to the Middle East, Egypt, the Indus Valley in India, and parts of China. Elsewhere, in Europe, North and South America and much of Africa, societies based on cities came much later.

In western Europe, for example, it was only with the arrival of the Romans that cities and writing appeared. The Romans took over the area they called Gaul (modern France) in the 1st century B.C., some 3,000 years after the first cities were built in Mesopotamia. Today, people in some parts of the world lead successful traditional lifestyles, adapted to their environment, just like their prehistoric ancestors. But even they are affected by the decisions of governments and businesses based in the world's cities.

▼ 'UBAID HOUSE
Houses, like this one in modern Iraq, became larger and more complex in the 'Ubaid Period. They were still made of mud bricks, but had a large central hall, many smaller rooms, a staircase, and drainage into open gullies outside.

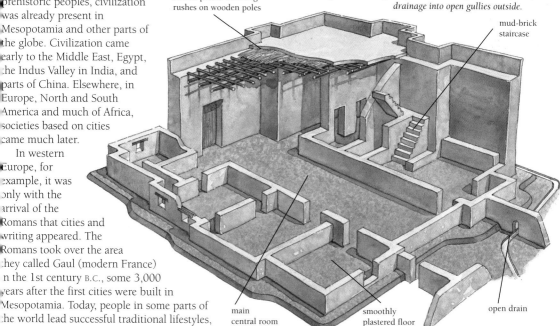

roof of plaster covering rushes on wooden poles

mud-brick staircase

main central room

smoothly plastered floor

open drain

▲ MARSH ARABS
These Marsh Arabs live in southeastern Iraq. They herd water buffalo and build houses out of reeds. This traditional lifestyle of the Marsh Arabs existed alongside the growing cities of Mesopotamia.

▼ ZIGGURAT
A Sumerian ziggurat consisted of a stepped platform made of sun-dried mud bricks. Only priests were allowed to climb to the top. An early example of a ziggurat is the White Temple of Uruk, made of whitewashed bricks, which dates back to the late 3000s B.C.

Key Dates

- 3500 B.C. The first cities are built in Mesopotamia. Among the most important are Uruk and Ur on the banks of the Euphrates River.

- 3200 B.C. Civilization spreads to Egypt.

- 3100 B.C. Writing is developed in and around the city of Uruk; people write on clay tablets.

- 2500 B.C. The first cities are built in the Indus Valley, Pakistan.

- 2300 B.C. Several of the Mesopotamian cities unite as a single kingdom under Sargon of Agade.

- 1800 B.C. Civilization develops separately in northern China.

Glossary

A

alignment Term used to describe objects that are lined up neatly. A stone alignment is a long row of standing stones, often lined up to correspond with the movements of the Sun, Moon, or stars.

alloy Material made by mixing two or more metals. The most common alloy in prehistoric times was bronze, made from copper and tin.

archaeologists People who study the buildings, tools, pots, and other remains of societies. They dig in the ground looking for objects that provide evidence of how people lived in the past.

archaic Term describing the early stages of development of a species or people. Archaic *Homo sapiens* refers to the remains of our own species that are similar to those of other early hominids.

australopithecine Member of the genus *Australopithecus*, a group of hominids that were alive more than a million years ago. They were smaller than later hominids, could stand upright, and probably used simple tools.

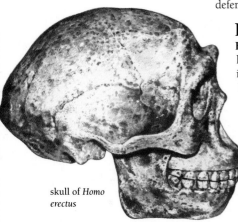

skull of *Homo erectus*

B

Bronze Age Period in which the use of bronze for making tools and weapons is well established. The Bronze Age occurs at different times in different parts of the world, according to when the alloy was discovered. There was no Bronze Age in the Americas.

burial mound Artificial earth mound containing the graves of one or more people.

C

casting Method of making bronze or iron objects by pouring molten metal into a mold.

Celts People who lived in central and western Europe during the Iron Age, just before these areas were occupied by the Romans.

coiling Technique for making pottery, in which long snake-like coils of clay are wound together and smoothed to make a vessel.

E

earthwork Bank or rampart made of earth. They were usually for defensive purposes.

F

Fertile Crescent Area, shaped like a crescent on the map, including modern Israel, Palestine, Syria, and parts of Turkey, Iran, and Iraq. This was the area in which farming was first established.

fossils Part of an animal or plant that is preserved in stone.

burial scene at Mehrgarh in India

G

genus A group of animals or plants that have characteristics in common. A genus normally has more than one species.

glaze Layer of material spread onto the sides of a pot before firing to create a hard, decorative, non-absorbent finish.

H

Halstatt Term for the first stage of the Iron Age in Europe, named after an Iron Age site in Austria.

hominid Member of the family *Hominidae*, which includes humans and other related species such as the australopithecines.

Homo erectus Form of human ancestor, which lived more than 500,000 years ago, walked upright, used stone tools such as hand axes, and probably used fire.

Homo habilis Early member of the human genus *Homo*, alive in Africa about 1.7 million years ago, which made simple pebble tools.

Homo sapiens The modern human species to which we belong. *Homo sapiens* developed around 100,000 years ago and by 35,000 years ago was the only hominid alive on Earth.

hunter-gatherers People who live on meat which they hunt and plants which they gather.

ce Age Period during which the
emperature was much lower than
oday, and when large parts of the
arth's surface were covered in ice
nd snow. There have been several
ce ages, but the one that affected
nodern humans was at its height
etween 30,000 and 12,000B.C.

ron Age Period during which iron
ecame the main metal used for
roducing tools and weapons. In
nany places, iron gradually
eplaced bronze, but in the
mericas and most of Africa, iron
vas the first metal to be used in
nis way.

a Tène Style of art produced by
ne Celtic peoples of Europe,
nown for its use of beautiful
urved and abstract designs.

nd bridge Area of land
onnecting two landmasses that are
ow separate.

M

egalith Large stone, either
anding on its own or used as part
f a tomb, stone circle, or other
nonument.

esolithic The Middle Stone Age.
he period during the Stone Age
when people improved their
unting techniques and began to
ake smaller stone tools.

esopotamia The fertile area
etween the Tigris and
uphrates rivers in what is
ow Iraq, where the earliest
vilizations began.

icrolith Very small
one cutting blade, often
ted into a wooden
andle, typical of the
esolithic period.

gazelle
rock art

N

Neanderthal Early hominid, very
similar to humans, but shorter
and stockier in appearance.
Neanderthals lived in Europe
and the Middle East, and died
out around 35,000B.C.

Neolithic The New Stone Age. The
period when people began to farm
but were still using stone tools.

O

obsidian Naturally occurring glass-
like substance formed in volcanoes.
Used in the same way as flint for
making tools.

ore Rock containing
deposits of metal.

P

Paleolithic The Old Stone Age. The
period when human life first
emerged. This time was typified by
a hunter-gatherer way of life and by
the use of simple stone tools.

paleontologist A person who
studies fossils.

prehistoric Period before people
learned to write and keep their
own historical records. The dates
of the prehistoric period vary in
different places around the world
depending on when people began
to develop writing.

pressure flaking The removal of
small pieces of stone from the edge
of a tool by pushing with a piece of
bone or antler. Pressure flaking can
produce a finely worked, razor-
sharp edge.

woolly
rhino

S

scraper Tool used for cleaning
animal skins or for carving.

Stone Age Term describing any
period when people made
their tools and weapons
out of stone.

Woman using a
scraper to prepare
skins for use as
clothing and
blankets.

Index

A

Africa
  civilization 61
  farming 50
  hominids 10–11, 12–13, 19
  hunter-gatherers 12–13, 50, 51
  iron 59
  post-Ice Age 32–3, 50
  rock art 34–5, 38
America 28–9, 38, 39, 48–9
animals
  in art 24, 25, 34–5, 38, 40
  dogs 29, 31, 33, 39
  farming 36, 38, 39, 44, 46, 49
  as food 12, 18, 20, 22, 30, 32
  skins 19, 21, 32, 33
archaeologists 8–9, 41
art
  cave paintings 20–1, 24–5
  Mesopotamia 60
  rock 26, 27, 34–5, 38, 51
Asia
  civilization 61
  farming 37, 38, 39, 46–7
  hominids 13, 14, 15, 18, 19
  Neanderthals 17
Australia 26–7, 35, 50–1
Australopithecines 10–11

B

boats 26, 27, 30, 49, 60
bone
  carvings 18, 22
  hominid 10, 11, 13, 16
  human 8–9, 41
  mammoth 7, 20, 22, 23, 33
  tools 20, 22, 24, 32, 56
  weapons 22, 24, 28, 29, 32
Britain 30, 31, 32, 54
bronze 52–3, 58
buildings 37, 40–1, 44–5, 46–7, 56–7, 60–1
burial 8–9, 16–17, 41, 47, 54

C

carvings 7, 18, 22, 24, 30, 41
Çatal Hüyük 40–1
caves
  Homo erectus 14, 15
  painting 20–1, 24, 25, 27, 35
Central America 48, 49
cereals 33, 36–9, 44, 46–7, 48
China 14, 15, 42, 43, 46–7, 59
civilization 60–1
Clovis culture 28, 29
copper 52–3
Cro-Magnons 20

D

dating methods 9

E

Europe
  Bronze Age 53
  civilization 61
  Cro-Magnons 20
  farming 38, 39, 44–5
  hominids 13, 14, 15, 19, 21
  Ice Age 22, 24–5, 31
  Iron Age 59
  lake villages 56–7
  megaliths 54–5
  Neanderthals 16, 17, 21

F

farming
  Africa 34–5, 50
  America 38, 39, 48–9
  Asia 38–9, 46–7
  Europe 38, 39, 44–5
  Middle East 33, 36–7
Fertile Crescent 36–7, 40, 60
fire 12–13, 22
fish 7, 22, 30, 51, 56
flint
  mines 30
  shaping 21, 33
  tools 13, 16, 20, 21, 23, 40
  weapons 28, 29
food
  hominids 10, 11, 12, 14
  Ice Age 28, 30, 40
forests 16, 30, 31
fossils 10, 11, 13, 28
France 14, 16, 20, 24, 25, 54
fruit 12, 30, 40, 47

G

goddess figures 24, 25, 41, 60
grave goods 8, 36, 47

H

hominids
  Homo erectus 12–13, 14
  Homo habilis 10–11
  Homo sapiens 18–19, 20–1
  Neanderthals 16–17
  spread 14–15
human figures 24, 34, 35, 41, 42, 44, 48, 60
hunter-gatherers 12–14, 18–19, 23, 30, 44, 50–1
hunting
  see also weapons
  hominids 11, 12, 13, 14, 15
  Homo sapiens 18, 19, 20, 22
  Ice Age 22
  paintings 34–5
  post-Ice Age 30, 31, 32

I

Ice Age 22–3, 24–5, 28, 29, 30–1
India 35, 46, 47, 58–9, 61
Iraq 16, 17, 60–1
iron 58–9
Israel 17, 18, 23, 33, 36
Italy 17, 45

J

jewelry 8, 26, 46, 51, 52–3, 57, 58, 60

L

lake villages 56–7
Leakey, Louis 10, 11

M

mammoths 7, 20, 22, 23, 28, 32
megaliths 54–5
Mesopotamia 60–1
metalworking 52–3, 58–9
Middle East 32–3, 36, 39, 41, 58

N

Neanderthals 16–17, 18
North America 28, 29, 30, 32, 48

P

painting
  Çatal Hüyük 40
  cave 20–1, 24–5, 27, 35
  materials 14, 25
  rock art 26, 29
plants 37, 38–9, 47, 48, 49
pottery 36, 41, 42–3, 44, 45, 46, 56, 60

R

religion
  Africa 34, 35
  Americas 48
  Australia 26, 35, 51
  Europe 21, 24, 32, 54–5
  Middle East 36, 41
rock art 26, 27, 34–5, 51

S

Scandinavia 30, 31
sculpture 20, 24, 36, 60
sea level 26, 30, 31, 33
shelters 7, 10, 14, 20, 23, 26, 29, 33
Siberia 28, 29, 30, 33
South America 28, 29, 34, 49
standing stones 54–5
stone tools
  Australia 27
  Cro-Magnons 20
  hominids 10, 11, 13, 14, 15
  Ice Age 30
  Neanderthal 16
  North America 28, 29, 32

T

tools
  Africa 50
  America 28, 29, 32
  Australia 27
  bone 20, 22, 24, 32, 56
  composite 20, 31
  Europe 20, 56
  farming 32, 37
  glass 27, 40, 51
  hominids 10, 11, 13, 14, 15
  Ice Age 30
  metal 53, 56, 58
  Neanderthal 16
  wooden 14, 15, 20
trade 40–1, 60
  Asia 46
  Australia 51
  Europe 31, 45, 57
  Ice Age 23
  Turkey 37, 39, 40–1, 45, 58

W

weapons
  bone 22, 24, 28, 29, 32
  development 6–7, 23, 24, 32, 48
  metal 53, 58
wood 14, 15, 20, 44–5, 56
writing 6, 60–1